75 *fun* FAT-QUARTER QUILTS

14 POPULAR DESIGNERS

13 QUILTS + 62 INNOVATIVE VARIATIONS

COMPILED BY ROXANE CERDA

C&T PUBLISHING

Text, photography, and artwork copyright © 2015 by C&T Publishing, Inc.

Publisher: Amy Marson

Creative Director: Gailen Runge

Art Director / Book Designer:
Kristy Zacharias

Editors: Lynn Koolish and
Monica Gyulai

Technical Editors: Priscilla Read and
Susan Nelsen

Production Coordinator:
Freesia Pearson Blizard

Production Editors: Katie Van Amburg
and Joanna Burgarino

Illustrator: Tim Manibusan

Photo Assistant: Mary Peyton Peppo

Style photography by Nissa Brehmer
and instructional photography
by Diane Pedersen, unless
otherwise noted

Published by C&T Publishing, Inc., P.O. Box 1456, Lafayette, CA 94549

Library of Congress Cataloging-in-Publication Data

75 fun fat-quarter quilts : 13 quilts + 62 innovative variations / compiled by
Roxane Cerda.

    pages cm

ISBN 978-1-61745-150-8 (soft cover)

1. Patchwork quilts. 2. Patchwork--Patterns. I. Cerda, Roxane. II. Title: Seventy-
five fun fat-quarter quilts.

TT835A1537 2015

746.46--dc23

                    2015012810

Printed in China

10 9 8 7 6 5 4 3 2 1

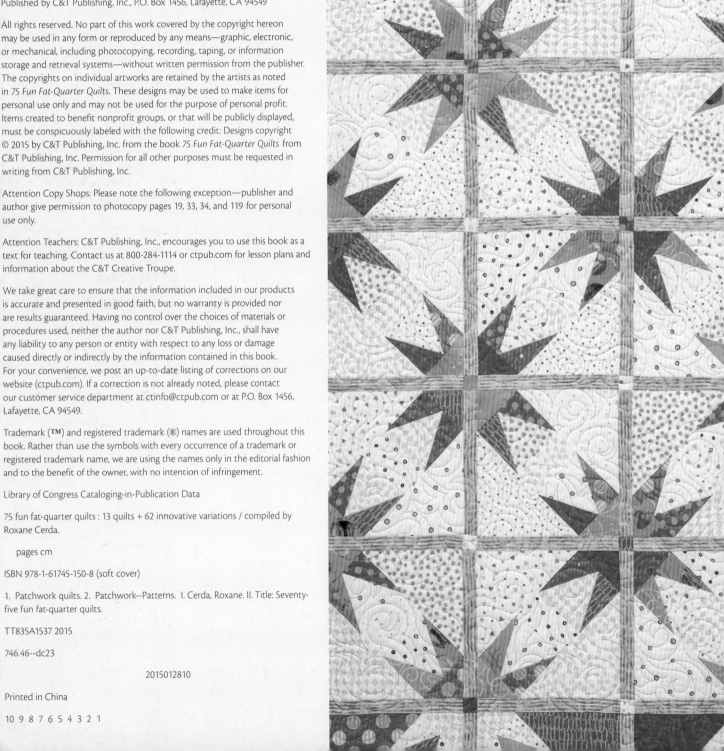

Contents

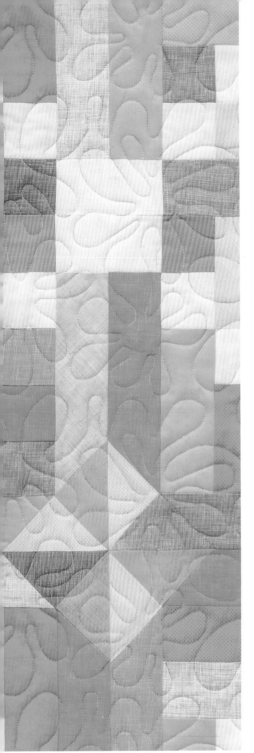

Introduction

Who among us hasn't been drawn to tantalizing piles of coordinated fat quarters? They really do look like candy, strung together in harmonic hues.

By dividing a yard of fabric into chunks instead of strips, we quilters have more options when cutting them apart for piecing. Indeed, when it comes to a quarter yard of fabric, fat beats skinny any day!

We asked fourteen inspiring quilters from around the country to design quilts that make the best of this unique cut of fabric. And they delivered. *75 Fun Fat-Quarter Quilts* presents an array of stunning quilt designs that range from modern to traditional, geometric to figurative, patchy to elegant.

Every chapter includes a main design and variations on it. By setting blocks on point or switching a high-contrast design to all neutrals or rotating some blocks 90°, a quilter can completely change the look of a project. Choose a favorite version to make with your own fat quarters, or find inspiration in the variations and create a new look based on the blocks presented.

With *Kim's Deal*, Jo Kramer and Kelli Hanken present seven different quilt designs based on one block, the Churn Dash block. In *Beaded Curtain*, Allegory Lanham combines rectangles and half-square triangles to make designs that look like beads, candies, and even Christmas crackers. In *Log Jam*, Kate Carlson Colleran manipulates a classic Log Cabin block and offers numerous electric designs that seem energized by their complementary color schemes.

Take a tour of these brightly illustrated projects and find plenty of reasons to dig into your own stash of fat quarters or scraps. Like eating candy, don't be surprised if it's hard to stop with just one.

FAT QUARTERS ARE 18″ × 20″ AND FABRIC IS 40″ WIDE UNLESS OTHERWISE NOTED IN A PROJECT.

Spring Petals Gone Graphic

MADE BY LIZ ANELOSKI

Spring Petals Gone Graphic is made of eight petal blocks 9″ × 9″ held together with simple, repeated center units. This flower section can be repeated four times on point or in a straight set to create a larger quilt, or the blocks can be used in a line to make a table runner. Mix and match the blocks to create a project featuring your favorite colors or fat quarters.

FINISHED BLOCK SIZE: 9″ × 9″ • FINISHED QUILT SIZE: 37½″ × 37½″

MATERIALS

Yardage is based on 42″ width.

- **Bright pink:** 2 fat quarters for Block A

- **Apricot:** 2 fat quarters for Block B and Unit C

- **White-with-black print:** 1 fat quarter for Unit C

- **Solid black:** 1 fat quarter for Block A and Unit C

- **Coordinating print:** 1 fat quarter for Center D

- **Black-with-white print:** 3 fat quarters for Block A, Block B, and Backgrounds E, F, and G

- **Binding:** ⅜ yard

- **Backing:** 42″ × 42″

- **Batting:** 42″ × 42″

CUTTING

WOF = width of fabric

BRIGHT PINK

- Cut 2 strips 9½" × 20".

  Subcut into 4 squares 9½" × 9½".

APRICOT

- Cut 2 strips 9½" × 20".

  Subcut into 4 squares 9½" × 9½".

  From the remaining fabric, cut 4 pieces 1½" × 3½".

WHITE-WITH-BLACK PRINT

- Cut 2 strips 3½" × 20".

  Subcut into 8 squares 3½" × 3½".

SOLID BLACK

- Cut 2 strips 3½" × 20".

  Subcut into 8 squares 3½" × 3½".

- Cut 1 strip 3½" × 20".

  Subcut into 8 pieces 1½" × 3½".

COORDINATING PRINT

- Cut 1 square 9½" × 9½".

BLACK-WITH-WHITE PRINT

See cutting diagrams.

- Cut 12 squares 3½" × 3½".

- Cut 4 pieces 2½" × 9½".

- Cut 4 pieces 5½" × 9½".

- Cut 4 pieces 5½" × 14½".

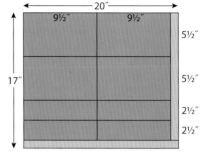

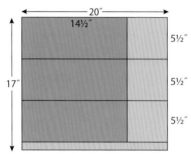
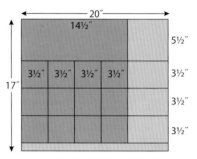

Cutting for black-with-white print

BINDING

- Cut 4 strips 2½" × WOF for double-fold binding.

INSTRUCTIONS

All seam allowances are ¼".

BLOCK ASSEMBLY

Mark a line from corner to corner on the wrong side of all the 3½" × 3½" squares.

Mark diagonal lines.

Block A

1. Place a marked white-with-black print square and a marked black-with-white print square on opposite corners of a large bright pink square, right sides together. Sew

just inside the line of each small square (see Sewing a Scant ¼" Seam, below). Trim, leaving a ¼" seam allowance. Make 4.

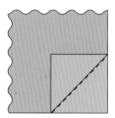
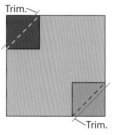

Sew and trim.

Sew just next to line.

Sewing a Scant ¼" Seam

Sew just inside the marked line (a thread's width toward the corner of the large square). This will allow for the thickness of the fold and will ensure that you don't end up with a short corner.

2. Press the small corners open. Trim each block to 9½″ × 9½″ if necessary. Make 4.

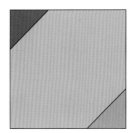

Block A

Block B

1. Place a marked white-with-black print square and a marked black-with-white print square on opposite corners of a large apricot square, right sides together. Sew just inside the line of each small square (see Sewing a Scant ¼″ Seam, page 6). Trim, leaving a ¼″ seam allowance. Make 4.

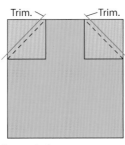

Sew and trim.

2. Press the small corners open. Trim each block to 9½″ × 9½″ if necessary. Make 4.

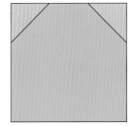

Block B

UNIT C

Sew a solid black strip on each side of an apricot strip. Sew a white-with-black print square on each side of this unit. Press. Make 4.

Unit C

CENTER SQUARE

1. Place a marked solid black square on each corner of the large coordinating print square, right sides together. Sew just inside the line of each small square (see Sewing a Scant ¼″ Seam, page 6). Trim, leaving a ¼″ seam allowance. Make 1.

Sew and trim.

2. Press the small corners open. Trim the block to 9½″ × 9½″ if necessary. Make 1.

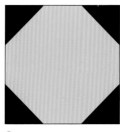

Center square

QUILT CONSTRUCTION

1. Refer to the quilt layout diagram (below) to arrange the blocks, units, and black-with-white print background pieces.

2. Sew together the pieces into rows. Press.

3. Sew together the rows. Press.

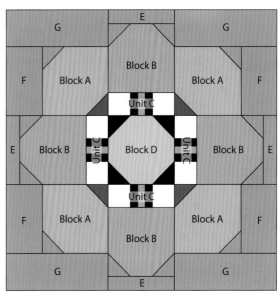

Spring Petals Gone Graphic quilt layout

QUILTING AND FINISHING

1. Mark quilting designs on the quilt top or plan to stitch without marking.

2. Layer the backing, batting, and quilt top. Use your preferred method to baste the 3 layers together.

3. Quilt as desired.

4. Bind the quilt.

On-Point Set with Corner Squares

FINISHED BLOCK SIZE: **9″ × 9″** • FINISHED QUILT SIZE: **53″ × 53″**

On-Point Set with Corner Squares quilt layout

MATERIALS

Yardage is based on 42″ width.

Follow the materials list for *Spring Petals Gone Graphic* (page 5).

ADD:

- **Apricot fabric:** 1½ yards for background corner squares

Replace the binding, backing, and batting with:

- **Binding fabric:** ½ yard
- **Backing:** 57″ × 57″
- **Batting:** 57″ × 57″

CUTTING

Follow the cutting instructions for *Spring Petals Gone Graphic* (page 6).

ADD:

- From the apricot, cut 2 squares 27″ × 27″; then cut each square diagonally once from corner to corner.

Replace the binding cutting with:

- Cut 6 strips 2½″ × WOF for double-fold binding.

INSTRUCTIONS

All seam allowances are ¼″.

1. Follow the Block Assembly instructions for *Spring Petals Gone Graphic* (page 6).

2. Add the background corner triangles. Press.

3. Follow the Quilting and Finishing instructions for *Spring Petals Gone Graphic* (page 7).

Straight Set with Borders

FINISHED BLOCK SIZE: 9″ × 9″ • FINISHED QUILT SIZE: 49½″ × 49½″

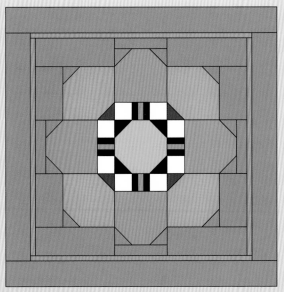

Straight Set with Borders quilt layout

MATERIALS

Yardage is based on 42″ width.

Follow the materials list for *Spring Petals Gone Graphic* (page 5).

ADD:

- **Inner border:** ¼ yard (You can use a fat quarter if you want to sew 2 shorter strips together to make the length needed for each border strip.)
- **Outer border:** 1⅛ yards

Replace the binding, backing, and batting with:

- **Binding:** ½ yard
- **Backing:** 54″ × 54″
- **Batting:** 54″ × 54″

CUTTING

Follow the cutting instructions for *Spring Petals Gone Graphic* (page 6).

ADD:

- Cut the inner border fabric into 4 strips 1½″ × WOF.

  Subcut into 2 rectangles 1½″ × 37½″ and 2 rectangles 1½″ × 39½″.

- Cut the outer border fabric into 5 strips 5½″ × WOF.

  Subcut into 2 rectangles 5½″ × 39½″ and 2 rectangles 5½″ × 49½″, piecing as needed.

Replace the binding cutting with:

- Cut 6 strips 2½″ × WOF for double-fold binding.

INSTRUCTIONS

All seam allowances are ¼″.

1. Follow the Block Assembly instructions for *Spring Petals Gone Graphic* (page 6).

2. Add the shorter inner border strips to the sides of the quilt top. Press. Then add the longer inner border strips to the top and bottom of the quilt top. Press.

3. Add the shorter outer border strips to the sides of the quilt top. Press. Then add the longer outer border strips to the top and bottom of the quilt top. Press.

4. Follow the Quilting and Finishing instructions for *Spring Petals Gone Graphic* (page 7).

Four On-Point Sets

FINISHED BLOCK SIZE: 9" × 9" • **FINISHED QUILT SIZE:** 105" × 105"

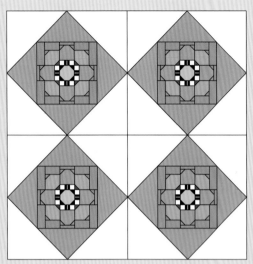

Four On-Point Sets quilt layout

MATERIALS

Yardage is based on 42" width.

- **Bright pink:** 8 fat quarters for Block A
- **Apricot:** 8 fat quarters for Block B and Unit C
- **White-with-black print:** 2 fat quarters for Unit C and 6¼ yards for background corner squares
- **Solid black:** 2 fat quarters for Block A and Unit C
- **Coordinating print:** 2 fat quarters for Center D
- **Black-with-white print:** 2¾ yards for Block A, Block B, and Backgrounds E, F, and G
- **Binding:** ⅞ yard
- **Backing:** 113" × 113"
- **Batting:** 113" × 113"

CUTTING

WOF = width of fabric

BRIGHT PINK

- Cut 8 strips 9½" × 20".

  Subcut into 16 squares 9½" × 9½".

APRICOT

- Cut 8 strips 9½" × 20".

  Subcut into 16 squares 9½" × 9½".

  From the remaining fabric, cut 16 pieces 1½" × 3½".

WHITE-WITH-BLACK PRINT

- Cut 7 strips 3½" × 20".

  Subcut into 32 squares 3½" × 3½".

- Cut 8 squares 27" × 27"; then cut each square diagonally once from corner to corner.

SOLID BLACK

- Cut 7 strips 3½" × 20".

  Subcut into 32 squares 3½" × 3½".

  From the remaining fabric, cut 32 rectangles 1½" × 3½".

COORDINATING PRINT

- Cut 2 strips 9½" × 20".

  Subcut into 4 squares 9½" × 9½".

BLACK-WITH-WHITE PRINT

- Cut 8 strips 5½" × WOF.

  Subcut into 16 rectangles 5½" × 14½".

  From the remaining strips, cut 8 rectangles 5½" × 9½".

- Cut 2 strips 5½" × WOF.

  Subcut into 8 rectangles 5½" × 9½".

- Cut 4 strips 3½" × WOF.

  Subcut into 48 squares 3½" × 3½".

- Cut 4 strips 2½" × WOF.

  Subcut into 16 rectangles 2½" × 9½".

BINDING

- Cut 11 strips 2½" × WOF for double-fold binding.

INSTRUCTIONS

All seam allowances are ¼".

1. Follow the Block Assembly instructions for *Spring Petals Gone Graphic* (page 6) and make 4.

2. Add the background corner triangles to each section. Press.

3. Refer to the *Four On-Point Sets* quilt layout (above) to arrange the sections.

4. Sew together the sections. Press.

5. Follow the Quilting and Finishing instructions for *Spring Petals Gone Graphic* (page 7).

Four Straight Sets

FINISHED BLOCK SIZE: 9" × 9" • FINISHED QUILT SIZE: 74½" × 74½"

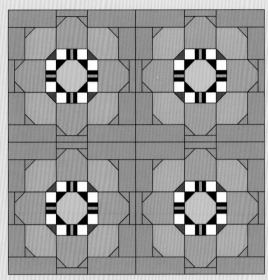

Four Straight Sets quilt layout

MATERIALS

Yardage is based on 42" width.

Follow the materials list for *Four On-Point Sets* (page 10).

Remove the fabric for the background triangles.

Replace the binding, backing and batting with:

- **Binding:** ⅝ yard
- **Backing:** 82" × 82"
- **Batting:** 82" × 82"

CUTTING

Follow the cutting list for *Four On-Point Sets* (page 10), except there are no background triangles.

Replace the binding cutting with:

- Cut 8 strips 2½" × WOF for double-fold binding.

INSTRUCTIONS

All seam allowances are ¼".

1. Follow the Block Assembly instructions for *Spring Petals Gone Graphic* (page 6) and make 4.

2. Refer to the *Four Straight Sets* quilt layout (above) to arrange the sections.

3. Sew together the sections. Press.

4. Follow the Quilting and Finishing instructions for *Spring Petals Gone Graphic* (page 7).

Table Runner

FINISHED BLOCK SIZE: 9" × 9" • FINISHED QUILT SIZE: 13½" × 79½"

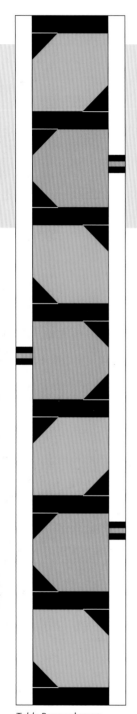

Table Runner layout

MATERIALS

Yardage is based on 42" width.

- **Bright pink:** 2 fat quarters for Block A

- **Apricot:** 2 fat quarters for Block B and Unit C

- **Solid black:** 2 fat quarters for Block A, Block B, Unit C, and sashing

- **Border:** ⅜ yard

- **Binding:** ½ yard

- **Backing:** 18" × 84"

- **Batting:** 18" × 84"

CUTTING

WOF = width of fabric

BRIGHT PINK

- Cut 2 strips 9½" × 20".

  Subcut into 4 squares 9½" × 9½".

APRICOT

- Cut 2 strips 9½" × 20".

  Subcut into 3 squares 9½" × 9½".

  From the remaining fabric, cut 3 rectangles 1½" × 2½".

SOLID BLACK

See cutting diagrams.

- Cut 14 squares 3½" × 3½".

- Cut 6 rectangles 1½" × 2½".

- Cut 8 rectangles 2½" × 9½".

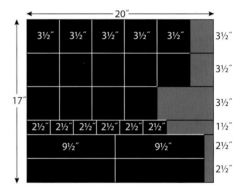

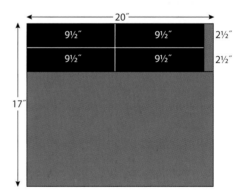

Cutting for solid black

BORDER

- Cut 1 strip 2½″ × 41½″.
- Cut 2 strips 2½″ × 38½″.
- Cut 1 strip 2½″ × WOF.

  Subcut into 2 strips 2½″ × 16½″.

BINDING

- Cut 5 strips 2½″ × WOF for double-fold binding.

INSTRUCTIONS

All seam allowances are ¼″.

BLOCKS

Follow the Block Assembly instructions for *Spring Petals Gone Graphic* (page 6) to make 4 of Block A and 3 of Block B.

UNIT C

Sew a 1½″ × 2½″ black strip to each side of a 1½″ × 2½″ apricot strip. Make 3 of Unit C.

BORDER

Arrange the C units and border strips to make 2 borders, referring to the illustration (page 12).

QUILT CONSTRUCTION

1. Refer to the illustration (page 12) to sew together the blocks and sashing. Press.

2. Add the borders. Press.

3. Follow the Quilting and Finishing instructions for *Spring Petals Gone Graphic* (page 7).

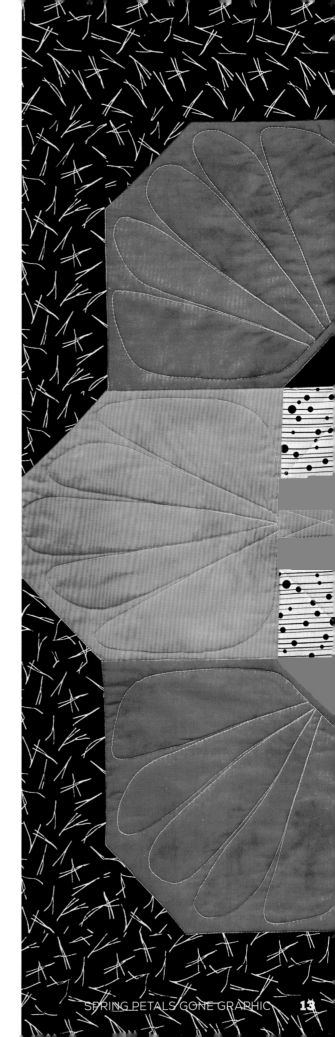

Straight-Set Blocks

FINISHED BLOCK SIZE: 9″ × 9″   •   FINISHED QUILT SIZE: 45½″ × 45½″

Straight-Set Blocks quilt layout

MATERIALS

Yardage is based on 42″ width.

- **Pink print:** 6 fat quarters for Block A
- **Orange stripe:** 7 fat quarters for Block B
- **Solid black:** 3 fat quarters for Blocks A and B
- **Binding:** ½ yard
- **Backing:** 50″ × 50″
- **Batting:** 50″ × 50″

CUTTING

WOF = width of fabric

PINK PRINT

- Cut 6 strips 9½″ × 20″.
  Subcut into 12 squares 9½″ × 9½″.

ORANGE STRIPE

- Cut 7 strips 9½″ × 20″.
  Subcut into 13 squares 9½″ × 9½″.

SOLID BLACK

- Cut 10 strips 3½″ × 20″.
  Subcut into 50 squares 3½″ × 3½″.

BINDING

- Cut 5 strips 2½″ × WOF for double-fold binding.

INSTRUCTIONS

All seam allowances are ¼″.

1. Follow the Block Assembly instructions for *Spring Petals Gone Graphic* Block A and Block B (page 6), noting the direction of the stripe. Make 12 Block A's and 13 Block B's.

2. Refer to the *Straight-Set Blocks* quilt layout (above) to arrange and sew together the blocks.

3. Follow the Quilting and Finishing instructions for *Spring Petals Gone Graphic* (page 7)

About the Designer

LIZ ANELOSKI loves designing bright, fun quilts that are just a step beyond traditional. She has been a senior developmental editor at C&T Publishing for more than two decades and is excited to see quilting grow and change as new quilters and companies add their creative designs, ideas, and products.

Lime in Da Coconut

Want Some Lime with That?

MADE BY CHARLOTTE ANGOTTI

FINISHED BLOCK SIZE: 6″ × 6″
FINISHED QUILT SIZE:

24½″ × 60½″ (Option 1, *Want Some Lime with That?*)
36½″ × 36½″ (Option 2, *A Twist of Lime*)

When I see lime green and white together, I just feel like singing, "Put the lime in the coconut and then you'll feel better." Here's a pattern that may look hard but actually is so easy that you can sing while you make it. This pattern has two options. The first, *Want Some Lime with That?*, is perfect as a bed runner for a queen-sized bed, which is all the rage in home decoration now. Option 2, *A Twist of Lime*, makes a great wallhanging.

MATERIALS

Yardage is based on 42″ width.

- **White:** 1 yard
- **Dark fabrics:** 6 fat quarters
- **Border and backing for Option 1:** 2 yards
- **Border for Option 2:** 1⅛ yards
- **Backing for Option 2:** 1⅛ yards
- **Binding:** ½ yard
- **Batting:** 29″ × 65″ for Option 1; 41″ × 41″ for Option 2
- **Tri-Recs tools** (optional)
- **Easy Angle or other half-square triangle tool** (optional)

CUTTING

WOF = width of fabric

Use patterns (page 19), Tri-Recs tools, the Easy Angle tool, or another half-square triangle tool.

WHITE

- Cut 8 strips 2½" × WOF. Subcut into:

  56 squares 2½" × 2½".

  56 half-square triangles using HST pattern or the Easy Angle triangle tool.

  52 Tri triangles using HST pattern or the 2½" line on the Tri tool.

- Cut 6 strips 1½" × WOF.

  Subcut into 12 strips 1½" × 20".

DARK

All of the fat quarters are cut exactly the same. Cut strips perpendicular to the selvage. Use the Recs pattern or the 2½" line on the Recs tool. When cutting the Recs and reverse Recs, fold the strip in half to cut the reverse units at the same time. You should have a total of 30 squares, 60 half-square triangles, 54 Recs triangles, and 54 reverse Recs triangles. There will be a few extra green pieces after completing the quilt.

From each fat quarter:

- Cut 3 strips 2½" × 20". Subcut into:

  5 squares 2½" × 2½".

  10 half-square triangles using the HST pattern or the Easy Angle triangle tool.

  9 Recs triangles and 9 reverse Recs triangles.

- Cut 2 strips 1½" × 20".

BORDER

- *Want Some Lime with That?* (Option 1): Remove the selvages from the fabric. Cut 3 strips 3½" × the length of the fabric. These pieces will be trimmed to fit the quilt after the top has been assembled. Reserve the remaining fabric for the backing.

- *A Twist of Lime* (Option 2): Remove the selvages from the fabric. Cut 4 strips 3½" × the length of the fabric. These pieces will be trimmed to fit the quilt after the top has been assembled.

BINDING

- *Want Some Lime with That?* (Option 1): Cut 5 strips 2½" × WOF for double-fold binding.

- *A Twist of Lime* (Option 2): Cut 4 strips 2½" × WOF for double-fold binding.

INSTRUCTIONS

All seam allowances are ¼".

BLOCK ASSEMBLY

Throughout the block assembly, use the fabrics randomly, paying attention only to whether it is a green or a white piece.

Star Blocks

1. Sew a green Recs triangle to a white Tri triangle. Press the seam allowances toward the green Recs. Sew a green reverse Recs triangle to the opposite side of the Tri triangle to complete the Tri-Recs unit. Press the seam allowances toward the reverse Recs. Make 52.

Tri-Recs units:
Make 52.

2. Sew each white 1½" × 20" strip to a green 1½" × 20" strip. Press the seam allowances toward the green. Crosscut the strip sets into 1½" × 2½" sections. Make 104.

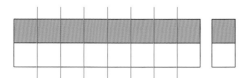

Crosscut into 9 sections.

3. Piece together the sections from Step 2 to make four-patch units. Make 52.

Four-patch unit:
Make 52.

4. Use 4 Tri-Recs units, 4 four-patch units, and 1 green 2½" × 2½" square to make a Star block. Be careful to orient the four-patch units correctly. Press the seam allowances of the top and bottom rows toward the four-patches. Press the seam allowances of the middle row toward the square. After the rows have been sewn to each other, press the seam allowances away from the middle row. Repeat this step to make 13 Star blocks.

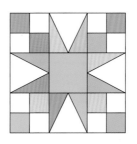

Star block:
Make 13.

Shoofly Blocks

1. Sew a white half-square triangle to a green half-square triangle to make a half-square triangle unit. Press the seam allowances toward the green. Make 56 units.

Half-square triangle unit:
Make 56.

2. Use 4 half-square triangle units, 4 white 2½" squares, and 1 green 2½" square to make a Shoofly block. Press the seam allowances toward the squares in all rows. After the rows have been sewn to each other, press the seam allowances toward the middle row. Make 14 Shoofly blocks.

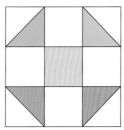

Shoofly block:
Make 14.

Want Some Lime with That?

1. Alternate and arrange the blocks into 9 horizontal rows of 3 blocks, beginning in the upper left corner with a Shoofly block. Sew the blocks into rows. Press the seam allowances toward the Shoofly blocks. Sew the rows together. Press the seam allowances to one side.

2. Trim 2 border pieces to fit the length of the quilt. Attach a border to each side. Press the seam allowances toward the borders.

3. Use the third border strip to cut 2 pieces to fit the width of the quilt. Attach one to the top and the other to the bottom of the quilt. Press the seam allowances toward the borders.

Want Some Lime with That? quilt layout

A Twist of Lime

1. Alternate and arrange the blocks into 5 horizontal rows of 5 blocks, beginning in the upper left corner with a Shoofly block. There will be one of each block left over. Sew the blocks into rows. Press the seam allowances toward the Shoofly blocks. Sew together the rows. Press the seam allowances to one side.

2. Trim 2 border pieces to fit the length of the quilt. Attach one to each side. Press the seam allowances toward the borders.

3. Trim the remaining 2 borders to fit the width of the quilt. Attach one to the top and the other to the bottom of the quilt. Press the seam allowances toward the borders.

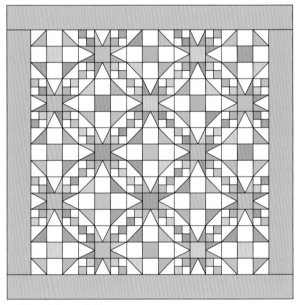

A Twist of Lime quilt layout

QUILTING AND FINISHING

1. Mark quilting designs on the quilt top or plan to stitch without marking.

2. Layer the backing, batting, and quilt top. Use your preferred method to baste together the 3 layers.

3. Quilt as desired.

4. Bind the quilt.

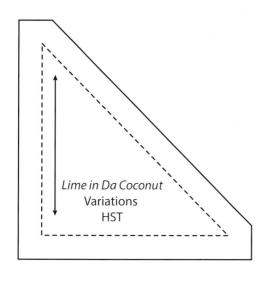

Lime in Da Coconut
Variations
HST

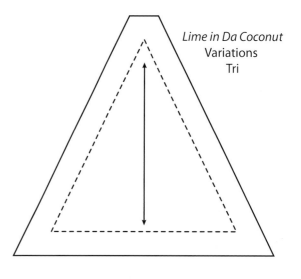

Lime in Da Coconut
Variations
Tri

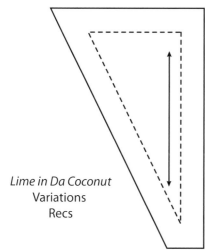

Lime in Da Coconut
Variations
Recs

About the Designer

Photo by Mike Clark, Chesapeake, VA

CHARLOTTE ANGOTTI teaches quilting internationally and lives in South Carolina. She holds a bachelor of arts degree in fine arts, speech, drama, and secondary teaching from Huntingdon College in Montgomery, Alabama, and found a career that put all those skills to good use.

She owned Quilt Works, a shop in Virginia Beach, Virginia, from 1981 to 1999, and now teaches quilting full-time. Many of her classes involve the use of her laser-cut kits, which enable students to get to work quickly. Known for her humor and use of color, Charlotte describes her career this way: "My hobby is making quilts. My job is making others like it as much as I do."

Farmhouse

MADE BY JERA BRANDVIG

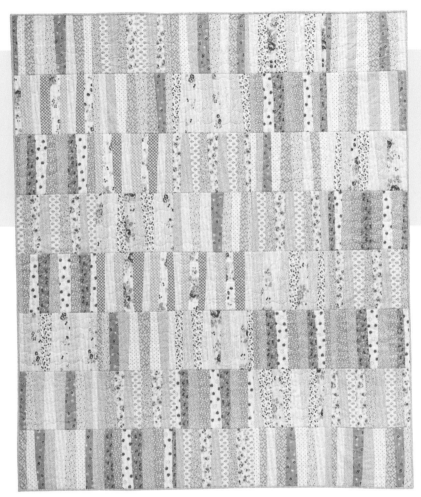

This quilt comes together really fast by stacking fabric pieces and cutting multiple strips at once. Nearly every bit of your fat quarters makes it into this no-waste quilt. You can also use the quilt-as-you-go method. Enjoy!

MATERIALS

- **Assorted colors:** 20 fat quarters
- **Backing:** 4 yards
- **Binding:** ⅝ yard
- **Batting:**

  Traditional layering method: 74″ × 88″

  Quilt-as-you-go method (see Quilt-As-You-Go, page 22): 90″ × 90″ (Batting must be needle-punched and at least 80% cotton.)

FINISHED BLOCK SIZE: 13½″ × 9½″   •   FINISHED QUILT SIZE: 68″ × 77½″

CUTTING

WOF = width of fabric

FAT QUARTERS

1. Divide the 20 fat quarters into 5 piles with 4 fat quarters per pile. Try to make sure that each pile includes lights and darks, as well as large and small prints.

2. Take a pile of 4 fat quarters and press them flat. Trim the fat quarters to 18″ × 21″ and then cut them in half, so that each fat quarter yields 2 rectangles 18″ × 10½″. Repeat this step for all 20 fat quarters.

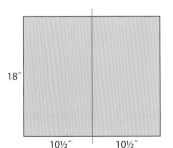

Trim fat quarters.

18″

10½″   10½″

3. Stack 4 rectangles 18″ × 10½″ directly on top of one another and press them to align all the edges. Use a rotary cutter and ruler to make 8 slightly tilted cuts. This will yield 9 stacks with 4 "wonky" strips per stack.

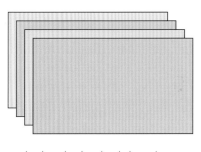

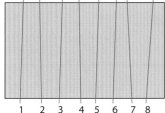

Stack rectangles and make "wonky" strips.

4. To assemble a block, take 1 strip from each stack from Step 3. Repeat, taking 1 strip from each stack. Arrange the strips in the same order and top-to-bottom orientation that they were in Step 3. (*The first strip should be from stack 1, the second strip should be from stack 2, and so on.*)

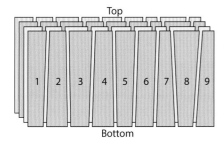

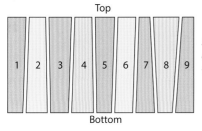

Assemble strips, one from each fabric stack.

tip **After you stack the strips that will form each block, pin them together into sets to keep them in order. Line up these sets near your sewing machine so they're ready to assemble.**

5. Repeat Step 4 for the remaining strips from Step 3. Then repeat Steps 2–4 for the remaining fat quarters. Make 40 strip sets.

BINDING

- Cut 8 strips 2½″ × WOF for double-fold binding.

BATTING

- If using the quilt-as-you-go method, cut batting into 40 rectangles 11″ × 15″.

INSTRUCTIONS

All seam allowances are ¼″.

1. Assemble strippy blocks from each pile of 9 strips. With right sides facing, sew together the strips and press open the seams. Make 40 blocks.

2. Square-up the blocks so each measures 10″ × 14″. To do this, place a block on a cutting mat and trim an edge so that 2 perpendicular sides form a 90° angle. Then use the cutting mat as a measurement guide and trim the remaining 2 sides so that the block measures 10″ × 14.″ *Note: Quilt the assembled blocks onto batting before squaring-up if you're using the technique explained in Quilt-As-You-Go (page 22). Square up after quilting.*

QUILT CONSTRUCTION

Farmhouse quilt layout

1. Arrange the blocks 5 across and 8 down.

2. Sew together 5 blocks to form a row. Repeat until you have 8 rows.

3. Sew together 8 rows to form the quilt top.

QUILTING AND FINISHING

For traditional finishing, follow these steps. To use the quilt-as-you-go method, see Quilt-As-You-Go (at right).

1. Cut the backing fabric in half across the width of fabric to yield 2 rectangles 42" × 72". Sew together along a 72" length. Press.

2. Layer the backing, batting, and quilt top. Use your preferred method to baste together the 3 layers.

3. Quilt as desired.

4. Bind the quilt.

Quilt-As-You-Go

I finished my *Farmhouse* using a quilt-as-you-go technique, though you can finish yours using any method you like. I like to use the quilt-as-you-go method because I can work on smaller, more manageable quilt sections while quilting. Once all the blocks are quilted, I sew them together, add the backing, and bind. You can learn about more ways to do this, as well as additional tips and tricks, in my book *Quilt As-You-Go Made Modern*.

If you want to quilt your *Farmhouse* as-you-go, begin by assembling the blocks as instructed. Before squaring-up the blocks, quilt them directly onto batting squares 11" × 15" (use needle-punched batting that contains at least 80% cotton). Quilt the blocks however you choose and have fun doing so! It's easier to accomplish intricate quilting on smaller batting blocks rather than on a full-size quilt. I quilted simple wavy lines using a straight stitch.

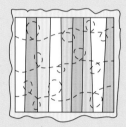

Quilt each block before assembling the quilt top.

When you are finished quilting, square-up all 40 blocks so they measure 10" × 14".

Sew together the quilted blocks as you would with a traditional quilt, using a ¼" seam allowance. Press open the seams and then clip the corners at an angle to reduce bulk at the intersections.

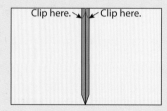

Clip here. ↘ ↙ Clip here.

Clip the corners of the seam at an angle.

Sew together the rows and press open the seams. Flip over the quilt and quickly press it with a warm iron to help flatten the seams.

Prepare the backing as instructed for a traditional quilt. Basting is quick since you already finished all your main quilting; simply place pins at the intersections to keep together the top and backing.

To attach the backing to my *Farmhouse*, I decided to stitch-in-the-ditch. I recommend using a neutral-colored thread and sewing slowly at first. Once you get the hang of it, you can go faster.

Cherry Pie

FINISHED BLOCK SIZE: 13½" × 13½" • FINISHED QUILT SIZE: 68" × 81½"

Cherry Pie quilt layout

INSTRUCTIONS

All seam allowances are ¼".

1. Make 30 blocks from the strip set piles as directed in the *Farmhouse* instructions (page 21). Trim each block to 10" × 14".

2. Add 2 solid 2½" × 14" rectangles to the top and bottom of each strippy block so that it measures 14" × 14".

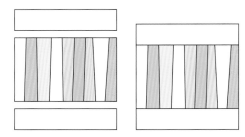

Add solid strips to top and bottom of blocks.

3. Arrange the blocks in a 5 × 6 formation, making sure to rotate every other block. Follow the Quilting and Finishing instructions for *Farmhouse* (page 22).

MATERIALS

Follow the materials list for *Farmhouse* (page 20).

Replace the 20 fat quarters, backing, and batting with:

- **Quilt top:** 15 fat quarters and 1½ yards solid fabric
- **Backing:** 5 yards
- **Batting:** 74" × 88"

CUTTING

WOF = width of fabric

SOLID FABRIC

- Cut 20 strips 2½" × WOF.

  Subcut each strip into 3 rectangles 2½" × 14" (total of 60).

FAT QUARTERS

- Cut strips from the 15 fat quarters following Steps 1–5 of the fat quarter cutting instructions for *Farmhouse* (page 20). Assemble 3 piles with 5 fat quarters per pile.

BATTING

- If using the quilt-as-you-go method, cut batting into 30 squares 15" × 15".

BINDING

- Cut 8 strips 2½" × WOF for double-fold binding.

Lazy Susan

FINISHED BLOCK SIZE: 13½″ × 9½″ • FINISHED QUILT SIZE: 68″ × 77½″

Lazy Susan quilt layout

Use just two colorways for a less scrappy and more traditional-looking quilt.

Follow the materials list from *Farmhouse* (page 20), except select 15 assorted red fat quarters and 5 white fat quarters.

Cut, assemble, and quilt as directed for *Farmhouse* (page 20).

Picket Fence 1

FINISHED BLOCK SIZE: 13½″ × 9½″ • FINISHED QUILT SIZE: 68″ × 74½″

Picket Fence 1 quilt layout

Follow the materials list and the cutting and piecing instructions from *Lazy Susan* (above).

QUILT CONSTRUCTION

To construct the quilt, cut 3 of the rows in half to create rows of varying heights:

1. After you've sewn together the 8 rows, take 3 of those rows and cut them in half horizontally to yield 3 shorter rows.

Cut 3 rows in half.

2. Assemble the quilt top, alternating short and tall rows.

3. Follow the Quilting and Finishing instructions for *Farmhouse* (page 22).

Picket Fence 2

FINISHED BLOCK SIZE: 13½″ × 9½″ • FINISHED QUILT SIZE: approximately 68″ × 80″

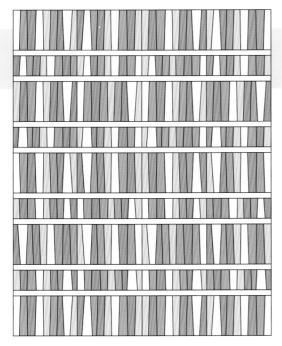

Picket Fence 2 quilt layout

Add solid strips between the alternating rows to give your quilt a different look.

MATERIALS

Fat quarters are based on 18″ × 20″ usable fabric. Yardage is based on 42″ width.

Follow the materials list for *Lazy Susan* (page 24).

ADD:

- **Solid fabric:** 1 yard

CUTTING

Follow the cutting instructions for *Farmhouse* (page 20).

ADD:

- From the solid fabric, cut 8 strips 2″ × WOF and 8 strips 2½″ × WOF.

QUILT CONSTRUCTION

1. Follow the Quilt Construction instructions for *Picket Fence 1* (page 24). Cut 2 rows into 4 short rows.

2. To subtly break up the rows, add narrow solid strips between each row. Sew together pairs of 2″- and 2½″-wide strips to make 8 long sashing strips.

3. Arrange and sew together 5 tall rows, 4 short rows, and the sashing strips, referring to the *Picket Fence 2* quilt layout (above). You will have a tall row left over. Trim the sashing.

Barnyard 1

FINISHED BLOCK SIZE: 8½″ × 8½″ • FINISHED QUILT SIZE: 68½″ × 85½″

Barnyard 1 quilt layout

Barnyard 2

You can also arrange the blocks from *Barnyard 1* so the strips run both vertically and horizontally, alternating the orientation of the blocks.

Barnyard 2 quilt layout

Make this variation with smaller blocks pieced from just four wonky strips.

Follow the materials list from *Farmhouse* (page 20).

CUTTING

Follow the cutting instructions for *Farmhouse* (page 20). In Step 2 of the fat quarter cutting instructions, cut the 18″ × 10½″ rectangle in half again so that it measures 9″ × 10½″. In Step 3, stack these smaller rectangles and make 3 tilted cuts. Continue with the rest of the cutting instructions.

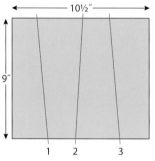

Make 3 tilted cuts.

INSTRUCTIONS

1. Follow the instructions for *Farmhouse* (page 20), but assemble strippy blocks from each stack of 4 strips and square them up so they measure 9″ × 9″. Make 80 blocks.

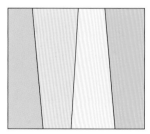

Assemble strippy blocks.

2. Arrange the blocks in an 8 × 10 formation.

3. Quilt and finish as described in *Farmhouse* (page 22).

Barnyard Stomp

FINISHED BLOCK SIZE: 8½″ × 8½″ • FINISHED QUILT SIZE: 68½″ × 85½″

Barnyard Stomp quilt layout

INSTRUCTIONS

1. Follow the instructions for *Barnyard 1* (page 26).

2. Arrange the blocks in an 8 × 10 formation, alternating solid and pieced blocks.

3. Quilt and finish as described in *Farmhouse* (page 22).

Alternate strippy blocks with a solid square for a completely different look.

MATERIALS

Follow the materials list for *Farmhouse* (page 20).

Replace 20 fat quarters with:

- 10 fat quarters and 2½ yards solid fabric

CUTTING

WOF = width of fabric

SOLID FABRIC

- Cut 10 strips 9″ × WOF.

  Subcut each strip into 4 squares 9″ × 9″. Make 40.

FAT QUARTERS

- Make 40 strippy blocks 9″ × 9″ as directed in the *Barnyard 1* cutting instructions (page 26).

About the Designer

Photo by Ben Brandvig

JERA BRANDVIG hails from the rainy city of Seattle. Her philosophy on quilting has always been to keep it simple, yet creative, and to have fun during the whole process; otherwise the unfinished projects may pile up. She is the author of *Quilt As-You-Go Made Modern* (from Stash Books, an imprint of C&T Publishing), which shows you how to break traditional quilting "rules" in a fun and creative way that works. Find out more on her website, Quilting in the Rain (quiltingintherain.com).

Pucker Power

DESIGNED AND PIECED BY DEBBIE CAFFREY
MACHINE QUILTED BY PHYLLIS KENT

MATERIALS

Fabric requirements for the small quilt are listed first, followed by the requirements for the large quilt in parentheses. It is a good idea to purchase a couple extra fat quarters of each value. There is little left over after cutting. The fabrics are used randomly; if the fat quarters are short, missing pieces can be cut from the extra fat quarters.

- **Light fabrics:** 8 (12) different fat quarters
- **Dark fabrics:** 8 (12) different fat quarters
- **Sashing:** 1 yard (1½ yards)
- **Border:** 1⅛ yards (1⅞ yards)
- **Binding:** ¾ yard (¾ yard)
- **Backing:** 3¾ yards (6 yards)
- **Batting:** twin (queen)
- **Thread to blend with fabrics for piecing**
- **Tri-Recs tools** (*optional*)

FINISHED BLOCK SIZE: 7½″ × 7½″ (small quilt) or 10″ × 10″ (large quilt)

FINISHED QUILT SIZE BEFORE BORDERS:
45½″ × 60½″ (small quilt) or 60½″ × 80½″ (large quilt)

FINISHED QUILT SIZE WITH SUGGESTED BORDERS:
54½″ × 69½″ (small quilt) or 72½″ × 92½″ (large quilt)

FINISHED QUILT SIZE WITH OPTIONAL SASHING AND SUGGESTED
BORDERS: 58¼″ × 74¾″ (small quilt) or 76¼″ × 97¾″ (large quilt)

CUTTING

WOF = width of fabric

Both light and dark fat quarters are cut the same way. Cut strips perpendicular to the selvage as shown in the cutting diagrams.

SMALL QUILT

FAT QUARTERS

Use the 3½" line on the Tri-Recs tool, or use the Tri and Recs patterns (pages 33 and 34). When cutting the Recs and reverse Recs, fold the strip in half to cut the reverse units at the same time.

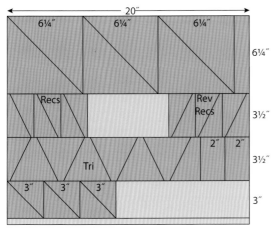

Fat quarter cutting diagram for small quilt

For each fat quarter:

- Cut 1 strip 6¼" × 20".

  Subcut into 3 squares 6¼" × 6¼". Cut each on the diagonal to make 6 half-square triangles.

- Cut 2 strips 3½" × 20".

  Subcut into 3 rectangles 2" × 3½", 6 Tri triangles, 6 Recs triangles, and 6 reverse Recs triangles.

- Cut 1 strip 3" × 20".

  Subcut into 3 squares 3" × 3". Cut each on the diagonal to make 6 half-square triangles.

- Cut 17 squares 1¼" × 1¼" from light fat quarter scraps.

- Cut 18 squares 1¼" × 1¼" from dark fat quarter scraps.

SASHING

- Cut 3 strips 8" × WOF.

  Subcut into 82 rectangles 1¼" × 8".

BORDER

- Remove the selvages and cut 7 strips 5" × WOF.

BINDING

The number of strips depends upon whether you add borders and/or sashing.

- Cut 6 or 8 strips 2½" × WOF for double-fold binding.

LARGE QUILT

FAT QUARTERS

Use the 4½" line on the Tri-Recs tool, or use the Tri and Recs patterns (page 33 and 34). When cutting the Recs and reverse Recs, fold the strip in half to cut the reverse units at the same time.

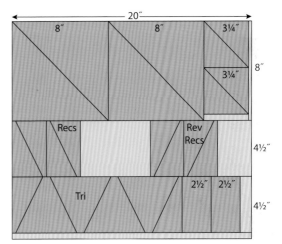

Fat quarter cutting diagram for large quilt

From each fat quarter:

- Cut 1 strip 8" wide.

  Subcut into 2 squares 8" × 8". Cut each on the diagonal once to make 4 half-square triangles.

  Subcut into 2 squares 3¾" × 3¾". Cut each on the diagonal once to make 4 half-square triangles.

- Cut 2 strips 4½" wide.

  Subcut into 2 rectangles 2½" × 4½", 4 Tri triangles, 4 Recs triangles, and 4 reverse Recs triangles.

- Cut 17 squares 1¼" × 1¼" from light fat quarter scraps.

- Cut 18 squares 1¼" × 1¼" from dark fat quarter scraps.

SASHING

- Cut 3 strips 10½" × WOF.

  Subcut into 82 rectangles 1¼" × 10½".

BORDER

- Remove the selvages and cut 9 strips 6½" × WOF.

BINDING

The number of strips depends upon whether you add borders and/or sashing.

- Cut 8 to 10 strips 2½" × WOF.

INSTRUCTIONS

All seam allowances are ¼".

BLOCK ASSEMBLY

Throughout the block assembly, use the fabrics randomly, paying attention only to whether the piece is a dark or a light value.

1. Sew a dark reverse Recs triangle to a light Tri triangle. Press the seam allowances toward the reverse Recs triangle. Add a dark Recs triangle to the second side of the Tri triangle. Press the seam allowances toward the Recs triangle. Make 48.

Light Tri-Recs unit: Make 48.

2. Sew a light reverse Recs triangle to a dark Tri triangle. Press the seam allowances toward the reverse Recs triangle. Add a light Recs triangle to the second side of the Tri triangle. Press the seam allowances toward the Recs triangle. Make 48.

Dark Tri-Recs unit: Make 48.

3. Sew a small half-square triangle to the top of each Tri-Recs unit. Use a light triangle on the units containing the light Recs and a dark triangle on the units containing the dark Recs. Press the seam allowances toward the half-square triangles.

Small half-square triangles added to Tri-Recs units

4. Sew a unit containing a light Tri triangle to both sides of each light rectangle. Sew a unit containing a dark Tri triangle to both sides of each dark rectangle. Press the seam allowances toward the rectangles. Make 24 of each.

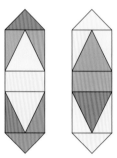

Sew Tri units to rectangles.

5. Sew a large light half-square triangle to both sides of a Tri unit that contains light Tri's and a light rectangle. Make 24 blocks. Sew a large dark half-square triangle to both sides of a Tri unit that contains dark Tri's and a dark rectangle. Press the seam allowances toward the large half-square triangles. Make 24 blocks.

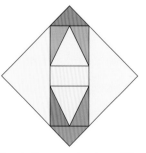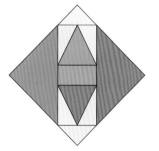

Sew half-square triangles to Tri units.

QUILT CONSTRUCTION

Pucker Power quilt layout

1. Arrange the blocks into 8 horizontal rows of 6 blocks each.

2. Sew together the quilt top by first piecing the horizontal rows. Press the seam allowances toward the sashing in each row. If the sashing has been omitted, press the seam allowances of the odd rows to the left and the seam allowances of the even rows to the right.

3. Sew together the rows. Press the seam allowances to one side.

BORDERS

Small Quilt

1. Sew together 2 border strips and trim to fit the length of the quilt. Repeat. Attach one to each side of the quilt. Press the seam allowances toward the borders.

2. Trim the remaining 2 border strips to fit the width of the quilt. Attach one to the top and the other to the bottom of the quilt.

Large Quilt

1. Trim 2 border strips to fit the width of the quilt. Attach one to the top and the other to the bottom of the quilt. Press the seam allowances toward the borders.

2. Sew together 2 border strips and trim to fit the length of the quilt. Attach one to each side. Press the seam allowances toward the borders.

QUILTING AND FINISHING

1. Mark quilting designs on the quilt top or plan to stitch without marking.

2. Layer the backing, batting, and quilt top. Use your preferred method to baste together the 3 layers.

3. Quilt as desired.

4. Bind the quilt.

Layout Options

There are seemingly countless ways to arrange the blocks. The quilt in the photo shows the blocks that are mostly dark around the perimeter, while the blocks that are mostly light are in the center. Try many different layouts before choosing one you like.

Here are some tips to keep in mind as you play with a layout:

• Sashing and cornerstones are optional. Include them if desired, but note that there are no sashing pieces or cornerstones around the quilt's outside edge.

• Audition different block arrangements before starting to sew.

• Use your camera to snap photos of each design before changing it.

• View all the variations on your computer and choose a favorite.

Some layout options

About the Designer

Photo by Mike Clark, Chesapeake, VA

Debbie Caffrey lives in New Mexico and teaches quilting around the country and internationally. She was born and raised in Peoria, Illinois, and lived for 22 years in Alaska, where she and her husband raised three children. Debbie began teaching more than 30 years ago and has been publishing books and patterns for 20 years. She offers adventurous quilters "mystery" patterns—designs that are delivered step by step so that the quilter doesn't know what the final design will be until the end. Reflecting on her career, Debbie recalls, "Once I was told never to make my job something I love because I would grow to hate it. But, I cannot imagine working at something I do not love." Visit Debbie at Debbie's Creative Moments (debbiescreativemoments.com).

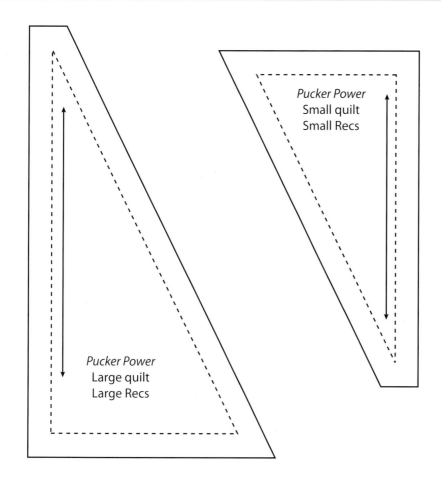

Pucker Power
Small quilt
Small Recs

Pucker Power
Large quilt
Large Recs

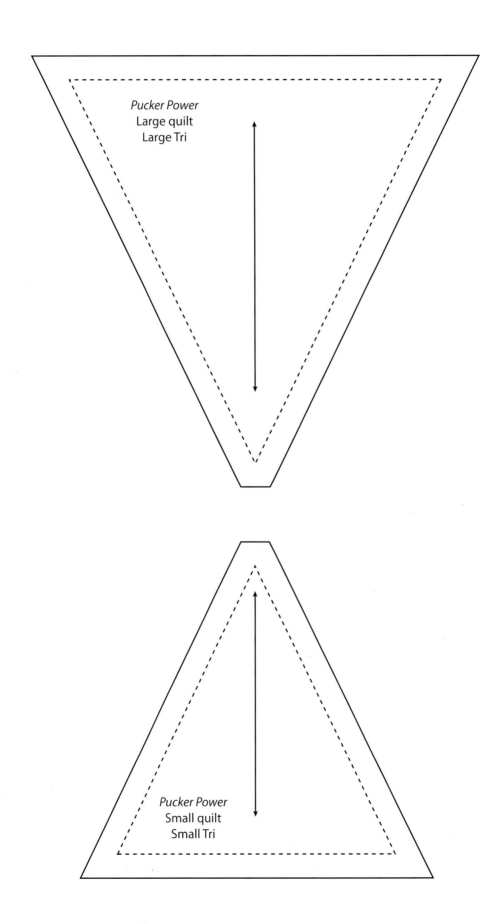

Pucker Power
Large quilt
Large Tri

Pucker Power
Small quilt
Small Tri

Tango

MADE BY AMANDA CASTOR

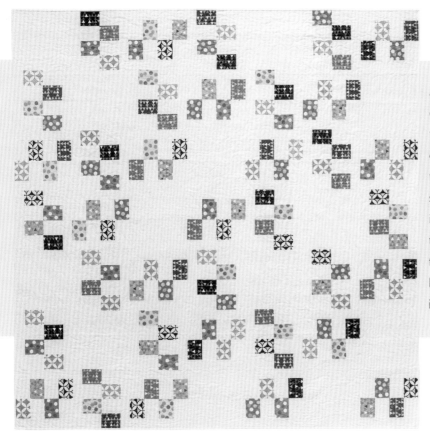

As a young girl, I always took dance classes and still love music and dance to this day. *Tango* reminds me of drawn-out dance steps that you try to follow when learning a new dance. Its simple patchwork block design makes it easy to assemble, and by just changing the colors and block layout, you can go from dance steps to rainbows or piano keys or even mind-bending optical illusions.

FINISHED BLOCK SIZE: 12″ × 12″ • FINISHED QUILT SIZE: 84½″ × 84½″

MATERIALS

- **Print fabrics:** 10 fat quarters
- **Background fabric:** 6 yards
- **Binding:** ⅞ yard
- **Backing:** 7½ yards
- **Batting:** 90″ × 90″

CUTTING

WOF = width of fabric

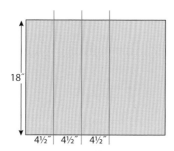

Fat quarter cutting diagram

PRINT FABRICS

- Cut 3 strips 4½″ × 18″ from each fat quarter.

BACKGROUND FABRIC

- Cut 4 strips 18″ × WOF.

  Subcut into 30 rectangles 4½″ × 18″.

- Cut 24 strips 2½″ × WOF.

  Subcut into 72 rectangles 2½″ × 12½″.

- Cut 5 strips 12½″ × WOF.

  Subcut into 13 squares 12½″ × 12½″.

BINDING

- Cut 9 strips 2½″ × WOF for double-fold binding.

INSTRUCTIONS

All seam allowances are ¼".

BLOCK ASSEMBLY

1. With right sides together, sew 1 print and 1 background rectangle 4½" × 18" along the 18" edge. Press the seams toward the print fabric. Make 30.

2. Repeat Step 1 for all 4½" × 18" rectangles.

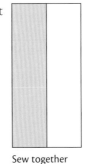

Sew together rectangles.

3. Cut each sewn rectangle set into 5 pieced units measuring 3½" × 8½". Make 144 pieced units.

3½"

3½"

3½"

3½"

3½"

Cut into pieced units.

4. Using a mix of prints, select 4 pieced units and sew them together into block sets. Alternate the placement of the print and solid. Make 36 block sets.

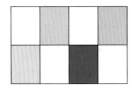

Block set

5. Sew a 2½" × 12½" rectangle onto each length of the block sets to complete the block. Make a total of 36 blocks measuring 12½" × 12½".

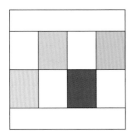

Tango block layout

QUILT CONSTRUCTION

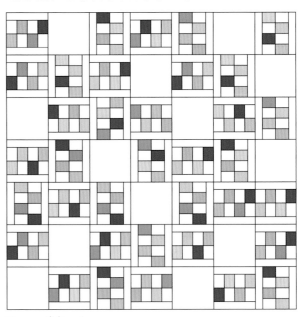

Tango quilt layout

1. Arrange all the pieced blocks and solid background blocks as shown in the quilt layout diagram.

2. Sew the blocks into rows. Press the seams in alternating directions for every other row.

3. Sew together the rows and press open the seams.

QUILTING AND FINISHING

1. Mark quilting designs on the quilt top or plan to stitch without marking.

2. Layer the backing, batting, and quilt top. Use your preferred method to baste together the 3 layers.

3. Quilt as desired.

4. Bind the quilt.

Rainbow

FINISHED BLOCK SIZE: 12" × 12" • FINISHED QUILT SIZE: 60½" × 72½"

Rainbow quilt layout

CUTTING

WOF = width of fabric

PRINT FABRICS

• Cut 4 strips 4½" × 18" from each fat quarter.

BACKGROUND FABRIC

• Cut 3 strips 18" × WOF.

   Subcut into 24 rectangles 4½" × 18".

• Cut 20 strips 2½" × WOF.

   Subcut into 60 rectangles 2½" × 12½".

BINDING

• Cut 7 strips 2½" × WOF for double-fold binding.

MATERIALS

• **Print fabrics:** 6 fat quarters (1 each of red, orange, yellow, green, blue, and purple)

• **Background fabric:** 3½ yards

• **Binding:** ⅝ yard • **Backing:** 3⅔ yards • **Batting:** 66" × 78"

INSTRUCTIONS

All seam allowances are ¼".

BLOCK ASSEMBLY

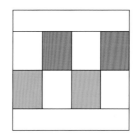

Rainbow block layout

1. Follow the instructions for *Tango* Block Assembly, Steps 1 and 2 (page 36).

2. Cut each sewn rectangle set into 5 pieced units, each measuring 3½" × 8½". Make 120.

3. Select 2 red and 2 orange pieced units and sew them together, alternating their orientation.

4. Make a total of 10 block sets in each color combination (red/orange, yellow/green, and blue/purple).

5. Sew a 2½" × 12½" rectangle onto each length of the block sets to complete the block. Make a total of 30 blocks measuring 12½" × 12½".

QUILT CONSTRUCTION

1. Arrange all the pieced blocks as shown in the *Rainbow* quilt layout diagram. Follow the instructions for *Tango* Quilt Construction (page 36).

2. Follow the Quilting and Finishing instructions for *Tango* Quilting and Finishing (page 36).

Alternating Blocks

FINISHED BLOCK SIZE: 12″ × 12″ • FINISHED QUILT SIZE: 66½″ × 78½″

Alternating Blocks quilt layout

CUTTING

WOF = width of fabric

PRINT FABRICS

- Cut 4 strips 4½″ × 18″ from each fat quarter.

BACKGROUND FABRIC

- Cut 3 strips 18″ × WOF.

  Subcut into 24 strips 4½″ × 18″.

- Cut 20 strips 2½″ × WOF.

  Subcut into 60 strips 2½″ × 12½″.

BORDER FABRIC

- Cut 8 strips 3½″ × WOF.

BINDING

- Cut 8 strips 2½″ × WOF for double-fold binding.

MATERIALS

- **Print fabrics:** 6 fat quarters (3 aqua and 3 orange)
- **Background fabric:** 3 yards
- **Border fabric:** 1 yard
- **Binding:** ⅝ yard
- **Backing:** 4 yards
- **Batting:** 72″ × 84″

INSTRUCTIONS

All seam allowances are ¼″.

BLOCK ASSEMBLY

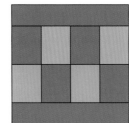

1. Follow the instructions for *Tango* Block Assembly, Steps 1 and 2 (page 36).

Alternating Blocks block diagram

2. Cut each rectangle set into 5 pieced units, 3½″ × 8½″. Make 120.

3. Sew together 2 aqua and 2 orange units. Make 30.

4. Sew a 2½″ × 12½″ rectangle onto each length of the block sets. Make a total of 30 blocks measuring 12½″ × 12½″.

QUILT CONSTRUCTION

1. Arrange the pieced blocks as shown in the quilt layout diagram. Follow the instructions for *Tango* Quilt Construction (page 36).

2. Piece 2 border strips 3½″ wide. Cut the strip to the length of your quilt top. Repeat to make a second pieced border. Sew the borders to each side of the quilt. Press toward the borders.

3. Repeat Step 2, this time cutting the pieced strips to the width of the quilt top. Sew the borders to the top and bottom of the quilt. Press toward the borders.

4. Follow the instructions for *Tango* Quilting and Finishing (page 36).

Zipper

FINISHED BLOCK SIZE: **12″ × 12″** • FINISHED QUILT SIZE: **66½″ × 66½″**

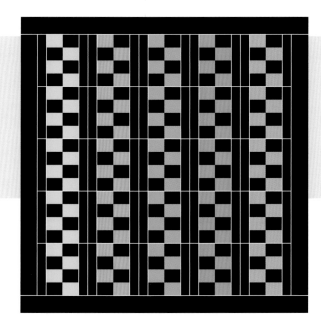

Zipper quilt layout

CUTTING

WOF = width of fabric

PRINT FABRICS

- Cut 4 strips 4½″ × 18″ from each fat quarter.

BACKGROUND FABRIC

- Cut 3 strips 18″ × WOF.

  Subcut into 20 strips 4½″ × 18″.

- Cut 17 strips 2½″ × WOF.

  Subcut into 50 strips 2½″ × 12½″.

BORDER FABRIC

- Cut 8 strips 3½″ × WOF.

BINDING

- Cut 8 strips 2½″ × WOF for double-fold binding.

MATERIALS

- **Print fabrics:** 5 fat quarters
- **Background fabric:** 3¼ yards
- **Border fabric:** 1 yard
- **Binding:** ⅝ yard
- **Backing:** 4 yards
- **Batting:** 72″ × 72″

INSTRUCTIONS

All seam allowances are ¼″.

BLOCK ASSEMBLY

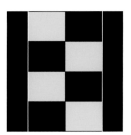

Zipper block diagram

1. Follow the instructions for *Tango* Block Assembly, Steps 1 and 2 (page 36).

2. Cut each sewn rectangle set into 5 pieced units, each measuring 3½″ × 8½″. Make 100.

3. Select 4 matching-color units and sew them together, alternating their orientation. Make 5 block sets for each print.

4. Sew a 2½″ × 12½″ rectangle onto each length of the block sets to complete the block. Make a total of 25 blocks measuring 12½″ × 12½″.

QUILT CONSTRUCTION

1. Arrange all the pieced blocks as shown in the *Zipper* quilt layout diagram. Follow the instructions for *Alternating Blocks* Quilt Construction (page 38).

2. Follow the instructions for *Tango* Quilting and Finishing (page 36).

Half-Sashed

FINISHED BLOCK SIZE: **12″ × 12″** • FINISHED QUILT SIZE: **76½″ × 80½″**

Half-Sashed quilt layout

MATERIALS

- **Print fabrics:** 6 fat quarters
- **Background fabric:** 3½ yards
- **Border fabric:** 1¼ yards   • **Backing:** 5 yards
- **Binding:** ¾ yard   • **Batting:** 82″ × 86″

INSTRUCTIONS

All seam allowances are ¼″.

BLOCK ASSEMBLY

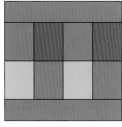

Half-Sashed
block diagram

1. Label the fat quarter fabrics A–F. Follow the instructions for *Tango* Block Assembly, Steps 1 and 2 (page 36).

2. Cut each sewn rectangle set into 5 pieced units measuring 3½″ × 8½″. Make 120 pieced units.

3. Select 2 color A and 2 color B units and sew them together, alternating their direction. Repeat this step to make a total of 10 block sets in each color combination (A/B, C/D, and E/F).

4. Sew a 2½″ × 12½″ rectangle onto each length of the block sets to complete the block. Make a total of 30 blocks measuring 12½″ × 12½″.

QUILT CONSTRUCTION

1. Arrange 5 rows with 5 blocks and 4 sashing strips per row as shown in the *Half-Sashed* quilt layout diagram. Follow the instructions for *Alternating Blocks* Quilt Construction (page 38), using 4½″ × WOF strips for the borders.

2. Follow the instructions for *Tango* Quilting and Finishing (page 36).

CUTTING

WOF = width of fabric

PRINT FABRICS

- Cut 4 strips 4½″ × 18″ from each fat quarter.

BACKGROUND FABRIC

- Cut 3 strips 18″ × WOF.

  Subcut into 24 strips 4½″ × 18″.

- Cut 28 strips 2½″ × WOF.

  Subcut into 84 strips 2½″ × 12½″ (60 for blocks and 24 for sashing).

BORDER FABRIC

- Cut 8 strips 4½″ × WOF.

BINDING

- Cut 8 strips 2½″ × WOF for double-fold binding.

Optical Illusion

FINISHED BLOCK SIZE: 12″ × 12″ • FINISHED QUILT SIZE: 48½″ × 60½″

Optical Illusion quilt layout

CUTTING

WOF = width of fabric

PRINT FABRICS

- Cut 4 strips 4½″ × 18″ from each fat quarter.

DARK GRAY

- Cut 1 strip 18″ × WOF.

  Subcut into 4 strips 4½″ × 18″.

- Cut 7 strips 2½″ × WOF.

  Subcut into 20 strips 2½″ × 12½″.

LIGHT GRAY

- Cut 1 strip 18″ × WOF.

  Subcut into 4 strips 4½″ × 18″.

- Cut 7 strips 2½″ × WOF.

  Subcut into 20 strips 2½″ × 12½″.

BINDING

- Cut 6 strips 2½″ × WOF for double-fold binding.

MATERIALS

- **Print fabrics:** 6 fat quarters

- **Dark gray:** 1¼ yards
- **Light gray:** 1¼ yards
- **Binding:** ½ yard

- **Backing:** 3 yards
- **Batting:** 54″ × 66″

INSTRUCTIONS

All seam allowances are ¼″.

BLOCK ASSEMBLY

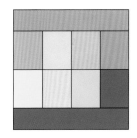

Optical Illusion block layout

1. Label the fat quarter fabrics A–F. With right sides together, sew together 1 color A and 1 color B 4½″ × 18″ rectangle along the 18″ edges. Press the seams toward the print fabric. Repeat for all the color A and B rectangles.

2. Repeat Step 1 to sew together C/D rectangles and E/F rectangles. Make a total of 4 pieced rectangle sets for each color combination (A/B, C/D, and E/F).

3. Sew together the light gray and dark gray rectangles as directed in Step 1. Make a total of 4 sewn rectangle sets.

4. Cut all the rectangle sets made in Steps 1 and 2 into 5 pieced units measuring 3½″ × 8½″. This will yield a total of 80 pieced units.

5. Select 1 strip set of each color combination from Step 4 and sew together as shown in the block layout diagram, keeping the light and dark gray unit on the right. Make 20 block sets.

6. Sew a light gray 2½″ × 12½″ rectangle onto the top of each block set and a dark gray 2½″ × 12½″ rectangle onto the bottom of each block set to complete the block.

7. Repeat Step 6 to make a total of 20 blocks measuring 12½″ × 12½″.

QUILT CONSTRUCTION

1. Arrange all the pieced blocks as shown in the *Optical Illusion* quilt layout diagram. Follow the instructions for *Tango* Quilt Construction (page 36).

2. Follow the instructions for *Tango* Quilting and Finishing (page 36).

Checkered

FINISHED BLOCK SIZE: **12″ × 12″** • FINISHED QUILT SIZE: **76½″ × 76½″**

Checkered quilt layout

MATERIALS

- **Print fabrics:** 5 fat quarters
- **White:** 3¼ yards for block background
- **Black:** 2⅞ yards for setting blocks and border
- **Binding:** ¾ yard   •   **Batting:** 82″ × 82″
- **Backing:** 4⅝ yards

CUTTING

WOF = width of fabric

PRINT FABRICS

- Cut 4 strips 4½″ × 18″ from each fat quarter.

WHITE

- Cut 3 strips 18″ × WOF.

  Subcut into 20 strips 4½″ × 18″.

- Cut 17 strips 2½″ × WOF.

  Subcut into 50 rectangles 2½″ × 12½″.

BLACK

- Cut 2 strips 18¼″ × WOF.

  Subcut into 3 squares 18¼″ × 18¼″.

- Cut 1 strip 9⅜″ × WOF.

  Subcut into 2 squares 9⅜″ × 9⅜″.

- Cut 8 strips 4½″ × WOF for the border.

BINDING

- Cut 9 strips 2½″ × WOF for double-fold binding.

INSTRUCTIONS

All seam allowances are ¼".

BLOCK ASSEMBLY

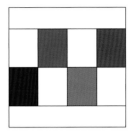

Checkered block layout

1. Follow *Tango* Block Assembly, Steps 1 and 2 (page 36).

2. Cut each sewn rectangle set into 5 pieced units measuring 3½" × 8½". Make 100 pieced units.

3. Using a mix of prints, select 4 pieced units and sew them together, alternating their orientation. Make 25.

4. Sew a white 2½" × 12½" rectangle onto each length of the block sets to complete the block.

5. Make a total of 25 blocks measuring 12½" × 12½".

6. Cut each 18¼" × 18¼" square across both diagonals to create 4 triangles per square. Make 12.

7. Cut each 9⅜" × 9⅜" square across one diagonal to create 2 triangles per square. Make a total of 4 triangles.

QUILT CONSTRUCTION

1. Arrange all the pieced blocks and solid background triangles on point as shown in the *Checkered* quilt layout diagram (page 42). The smaller background triangles will be in each corner.

2. Sew the blocks and setting triangles into diagonal rows, pressing the seams in alternating directions for every other row.

3. Sew together the rows and press open the seams.

4. Piece together 2 border strips 4½" wide. Cut the strip to the length of your quilt top. Repeat to make a second pieced border. Sew the borders to each side of the quilt. Press toward the borders.

5. Repeat Step 4, this time cutting the pieced strips to the width of the quilt top. Sew the borders to the top and bottom of the quilt. Press toward the borders.

6. Follow the instructions for *Tango* Quilting and Finishing (page 36).

About the Designer

Photo by Eric Lubrick, Eric Lubrick Photography

AMANDA CASTOR is a lover of fabric who has been quilting on and off for about fourteen years. Her designs tend to be based on traditional patchwork, but with a modern flair. Read all about her sewing adventures and see some of her other designs on her blog Material Girl (materialgirlquilts.wordpress.com).

Log Jam

DESIGNED AND PIECED BY KATE CARLSON COLLERAN
QUILTED BY CRYSTAL ZAGNOLI

I love quilt blocks that change the overall quilt pattern when you turn them around. And I love quilt blocks that create secondary patterns just by being placed next to each other. Log Jam is a block that does both! And it uses fat quarters—my favorite kind of precut.

With the Log Jam block you can make the main quilt or its variations. Add some more fat quarters and you can have two quilts instead of just one— *Log Jam* and its *Alter Ego*! There are even options to make the quilt bigger. The idea is to make it yours.

FINISHED BLOCK SIZE: 12″ × 12″ • FINISHED QUILT SIZE: 63½″ × 75½″

MATERIALS

- **Coral, orange, pink, and yellow:** total of 10 fat quarters
- **Blue and green:** 10 fat quarters
- **White:** 1 yard for background

- **Border:** ½ yard
- **Binding:** ⅝ yard
- **Backing:** 4⅝ yards
- **Batting:** 70″ × 82″

CUTTING

WOF = width of fabric

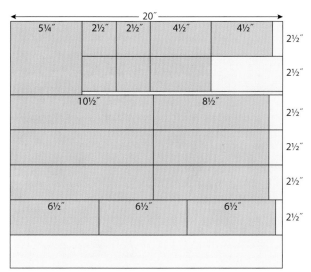

Fat quarter cutting diagram 1

Fat quarter cutting diagram 2

CORAL, ORANGE, PINK, AND YELLOW

- Cut 5 fat quarters following cutting diagram 1.

- Cut 5 fat quarters following cutting diagram 2.

In the coral group, you should have a total of 30 rectangles 2½″ × 10½″, 30 rectangles 2½″ × 8½″, 30 rectangles 2½″ × 6½″, 30 rectangles 2½″ × 4½″, 30 squares 2½″ × 2½″, and 15 squares 5¼″ × 5¼″. Cut the 5¼″ × 5¼″ squares on the diagonal twice to make 120 quarter-square triangles.

BLUE AND GREEN

- Cut 5 fat quarters following cutting diagram 1.

- Cut 5 fat quarters following cutting diagram 2.

In the blue group, you will have the same number of squares and rectangles as the coral group. Keep the 2 groups separate until you start to assemble the blocks.

> **tip** Here's a tip to speed up the process of cutting multiple fat quarters into the same dimensions: Unfold each fat quarter into a single layer. Stack three or four together and then cut them according to the diagrams. It will save a little time!

WHITE

- Cut 12 strips 2½″ × WOF.

  Subcut into 180 squares 2½″ × 2½″.

BORDER

- Cut 7 strips 2″ × WOF. Piece together with diagonal seams; then cut into 2 strips 2″ × 72½″ for the side borders and 2 strips 2″ × 63½″ for the top and bottom borders.

BINDING

- Cut 8 strips 2½″ × WOF for double-fold binding.

BACKING

- Cut 2 pieces 40″ × 82″. Piece them together and trim to about 70″ × 82″.

INSTRUCTIONS

All seam allowances are ¼". Follow the arrows for pressing suggestions. For a scrappy look, mix up the fat quarter fabrics as you sew together each block.

BLOCK ASSEMBLY

Refer to the Log Jam block layout diagram to make the rows. All rows for the block should measure 2½" × 10½".

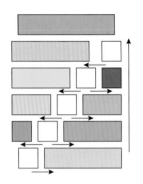

Log Jam block layout, Rows 1–6; press in direction of arrows.

1. Row 2: Sew a coral group 2½" × 8½" rectangle to a white 2½" × 2½" square.

2. Row 1: Sew a coral group 2½" × 10½" rectangle to the top of Row 2.

3. Row 3: Sew a coral group 2½" × 6½" rectangle to a white 2½" × 2½" square. Sew a blue group 2½" × 2½" square to the right side of the row. Sew Row 3 to the bottom of Row 2.

4. Row 4: Sew a coral group 2½" × 4½" rectangle to a white 2½" × 2½" square. Sew a blue group 2½" × 4½" rectangle to the right side of the row. Sew Row 4 to the bottom of Row 3.

5. Row 5: Sew a coral group 2½" × 2½" square to a white 2½" × 2½" square. Sew a blue group 2½" × 6½" rectangle to the right side of the row. Sew Row 5 to the bottom of Row 4.

6. Row 6: Sew a white 2½" × 2½" square to a blue group 2½" × 8½" rectangle. Sew Row 6 to the bottom of Row 5. The block should measure 10½" × 10½".

7. Sew a white 2½" × 2½" square to the top of a blue group 2½" × 10½" rectangle. Sew the unit to the right edge of the block. The block should measure 12½" × 12½".

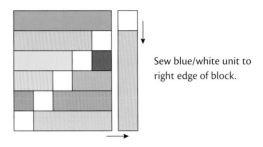

Sew blue/white unit to right edge of block.

8. Sew together 2 coral group triangles along their short edges. Make 30 coral triangle units. Repeat with the blue group triangles to make 30 blue triangle units.

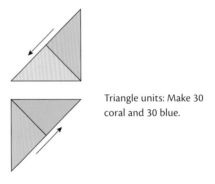

Triangle units: Make 30 coral and 30 blue.

9. On the block, measure 4½" from the blue corner along each side and make a mark as shown.

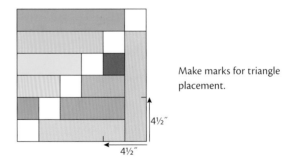

Make marks for triangle placement.

4½"

4½"

10. Position a coral triangle unit across the corner of the block with the point toward the center of the block. Line up the diagonal edge of the triangle with the marks you made. The triangle points will extend ¼" past the edge of the block. Sew the triangle to the block ¼" from the long edge of the triangle; your seam should start and stop at the marks. It's helpful to use a ¼" piecing foot on your sewing machine.

tip Here are a few pointers about adding the triangles: Because triangles have bias edges, it is easy to stretch them out of shape. Use a little spray starch to minimize stretching, and handle them very gently. If you don't have a ¼″ piecing foot, consider marking your sewing line with a disappearing marking pen. I found it helpful to line up the triangle unit's center seam allowance with the block's seam allowance and then gently adjust the edges to match the marks I made. A few pins will help hold the triangle unit in place while you sew the seam.

11. Trim the excess block even with the triangle's long edge. Press the triangle toward the corner of the block.

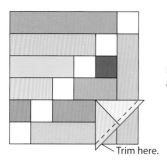

Press triangle toward corner of block.

Trim here.

tip Before trimming the block, fold the triangle toward the corner of the block and check that the triangle was sewn in the right spot!

12. Repeat Steps 9–11 on the opposite (coral) corner of the block with a blue triangle unit. The Log Jam block should measure 12½″ × 12½″. Make 30.

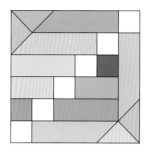

Completed Log Jam block: Make 30.

QUILT CONSTRUCTION

1. Refer to the quilt layout diagram to arrange all the blocks into 6 rows of 5 blocks each.

2. Sew together the blocks in each row. Alternate the pressing direction in each row. Then sew together the rows. The quilt top should measure 60½″ × 72½″.

3. Sew a 2″ × 72½″ border to each side of the quilt. Press the seams toward the borders.

4. Sew a 2″ × 63½″ border to the top and bottom of the quilt. Press toward the borders. The quilt top should measure 63½″ × 75½″.

Log Jam quilt layout

QUILTING AND FINISHING

1. Mark quilting designs on the quilt top or plan to stitch without marking.

2. Layer the backing, batting, and quilt top. Use your preferred method to baste together the 3 layers.

3. Quilt as desired.

4. Bind the quilt.

5. Label your quilt so everyone knows who made it!

I changed the look of the quilt by rotating the Log Jam blocks.

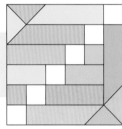

I switched up the block a bit by adding the blue triangle units to
the blue side of the blocks and the coral triangle units to the coral
side of the blocks.

Alter Ego

FINISHED BLOCK SIZE: 12" × 12" • FINISHED QUILT SIZE: 63½" × 75½"

Alter Ego quilt layout

So ... if you buy a few more fat quarters than needed to make the main *Log Jam* quilt, you can make two quilts! How cool is that? By following this expanded materials list and instructions, you will make both *Log Jam* and *Alter Ego*, its sister quilt.

MATERIALS

These amounts are enough for two quilts.

- **Coral, orange, pink, and yellow:** 15 fat quarters
- **Blue and green:** 15 fat quarters
- **White:** 4½ yards for background

- **Border:** 1 yard
- **Binding:** 1⅛ yards
- **Backing:** 9¼ yards
- **Batting:** 2 pieces 70" × 82"

CUTTING

WOF = width of fabric

The materials list is based on fat quarters with a cutting area of at least 16" × 20". If your fat quarters are not that big, you may need to get more fabric.

Fat quarter cutting diagram 3

CORAL, ORANGE, PINK, AND YELLOW

- Cut 15 fat quarters following cutting diagram 3.

In the coral group, you should have a total of 30 rectangles 2½" × 10½", 30 rectangles 2½" × 8½", 30 rectangles 2½" × 6½", 30 rectangles 2½" × 4½", 120 squares 2½" × 2½", and 30 squares 5¼" × 5¼". Cut the 5¼" × 5¼" squares on the diagonal twice to make 120 quarter-square triangles.

BLUE AND GREEN

- Cut 15 fat quarters following cutting diagram 3.

In the blue group, you will have the same number of squares and rectangles as the coral group. Keep the 2 groups separate until you start to assemble the blocks.

WHITE

- Cut 62 strips 2½″ × WOF.

  Subcut 12 strips into 180 squares 2½″ × 2½″ for *Log Jam* (Option 1). Cut the other 50 strips into 60 rectangles 2½″ × 10½″, 60 rectangles 2½″ × 8½″, 60 rectangles 2½″ × 6½″, 60 rectangles 2½″ × 4½″, and 60 squares 2½″ × 2½″ for *Alter Ego* (Option 2).

BORDER

- For each quilt, cut 7 strips 2″ × WOF. Subcut into 2 strips 2″ × 72½″ for side borders and 2 strips 2″ × 63½″ for top and bottom borders.

BINDING

- For each quilt, cut 8 strips 2½″ × WOF for double-fold binding.

BACKING

- For each quilt, cut 2 pieces 40″ × 82″. Piece them together and trim to about 70″ × 82″.

INSTRUCTIONS

These instructions are for the Alter Ego *quilt. For the* Log Jam *quilt, follow all the instructions for* Log Jam *(pages 44–48). All seam allowances are ¼″. Follow the arrows for pressing suggestions. For a scrappy look, mix up the fabrics as you sew together each block.*

BLOCK ASSEMBLY

Refer to the Alter Ego block layout diagram. Each row should measure 2½″ × 12½″. Make 30 blocks.

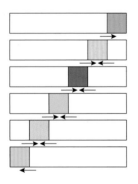

Alter Ego block layout, Rows 1–6

1. Row 1: Sew a white 2½″ × 10½″ rectangle to a blue group 2½″ × 2½″ square.

2. Row 2: Sew a white 2½″ × 8½″ rectangle to a coral group 2½″ × 2½″ square. Sew a white 2½″ × 2½″ square to the right side of the row.

3. Row 3: Sew a white 2½″ × 6½″ rectangle to a blue group 2½″ × 2½″ square. Sew a white 2½″ × 4½″ rectangle to the right side of the row.

4. Row 4: Sew a white 2½″ × 4½″ rectangle to a coral group square. Sew a white 2½″ × 6½″ rectangle to the right side of the row.

5. Row 5: Sew a white 2½″ × 2½″ square to a blue group 2½″ × 2½″ square. Sew a white 2½″ × 8½″ rectangle to the right side of the row.

6. Row 6: Sew a coral group 2½″ × 2½″ square to a white 2½″ × 10½″ rectangle.

7. Sew together the rows. The block should measure 12½″ × 12½″.

8. Follow *Log Jam* Block Assembly, Steps 8–11 (page 46). Complete the blocks by adding the corner triangles. Make 30 Alter Ego blocks.

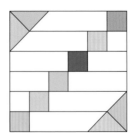

Alter Ego block: Make 30.

QUILT CONSTRUCTION

For both quilts, follow the instructions for *Log Jam* Quilt Construction (page 47).

QUILTING AND FINISHING

Follow the instructions for *Log Jam* Quilting and Finishing (page 47).

Off Line

Off Line quilt layout

Even a variation deserves a variation! For this twist on *Alter Ego*, you will substitute a blue rectangle for one of the white rectangles. I used the border fabric for these pieces. These instructions are for making one *Log Jam* quilt and one *Off Line* quilt. Double down!

MATERIALS

Follow the materials list for *Alter Ego* (page 49).

Reduce the white fabric to 4 yards.

Increase the blue border fabric to 1⅝ yards.

CUTTING

WOF = width of fabric

Follow the cutting instructions for Alter Ego *(page 49), but with these changes:*

WHITE

- Delete 10 strips and 30 rectangles 2½″ × 10½″.

BORDER

- Add 10 strips 2½″ × WOF and cut into 30 rectangles 2½″ × 10½″.

INSTRUCTIONS

There is a small change in the block assembly for *Off Line*. For everything else, follow the instructions for *Alter Ego* (page 49).

BLOCK ASSEMBLY

Refer to the Off Line block assembly diagram. Except for the changes listed, follow the instructions for Log Jam *Block Assembly (page 46).*

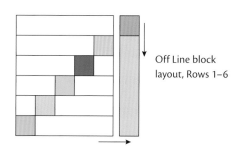

Off Line block layout, Rows 1–6

1. Substitute the coral and blue group rectangles for the white rectangles and alternate the coral group and blue group squares in each row, starting with a coral group square in Row 2.

2. For Step 7, use the blue group 2½″ × 10½″ rectangle with a blue group 2½″ × 2½″ square.

3. Follow *Log Jam* Block Assembly, Steps 8–11 (page 46). Complete the blocks by adding the corner triangles. The *Off Line* block should measure 12½″ × 12½″.

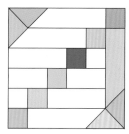

Off Line block layout

QUILT CONSTRUCTION

For both quilts, follow the instructions for *Log Jam* Quilt Construction (page 47).

QUILTING AND FINISHING

Follow the instructions for *Log Jam* Quilting and Finishing (page 47).

Third in Line

FINISHED BLOCK SIZE: **12" × 12"**   •   FINISHED QUILT SIZE: **75½" × 87½"**

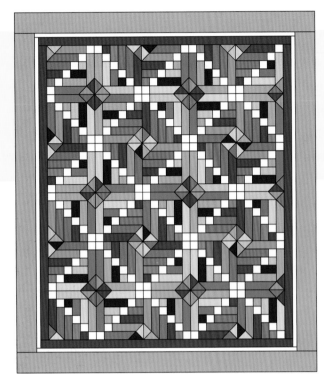

Third in Line quilt layout

Sometimes you want to make a quilt bigger than designed. Adding borders is an easy way to expand a quilt. For this *Log Jam* variation, you will make the same 30 blocks as in the main quilt, but you will then add a total of three borders. I also changed up the colors so you can see the quilt with a different look.

MATERIALS

- **Red:** 10 fat quarters
- **Black and gray:** total of 10 fat quarters
- **White:** 1 yard for background
- **Red inner border:** ⅝ yard (Border 1)
- **White middle border:** ½ yard (Border 2)
- **Dark gray outer border:** 1¼ yards (Border 3)
- **Black:** ⅝ yard for binding
- **Backing:** 7 yards
- **Batting:** 82" × 94"

CUTTING

WOF = width of fabric

Fat quarters assume a cutting area of 16" × 20". If your fat quarter does not have this amount, you may need to get more fabric.

RED, BLACK, GRAY, AND WHITE

- For the fat quarter fabrics and the white fabric, follow the instructions for *Log Jam* Cutting (page 45).

RED INNER BORDER

- Cut 8 strips 2½" × WOF and piece them together on the diagonal.

  Subcut into 2 strips 2½" × 72½" for the side borders and 2 strips 2½" × 64½" for the top and bottom borders.

WHITE MIDDLE BORDER

- Cut 8 strips 1¾" × WOF and piece them together on the diagonal.

  Subcut into 2 strips 1¾" × 76½" for the side borders and 2 strips 1¾" × 67" for the top and bottom borders.

DARK GRAY OUTER BORDER

- Cut 8 strips 4¾" × WOF and piece them together with straight seams.

  Subcut into 2 strips 4¾" × 79" for the side borders and 2 strips 4¾" × 75½" for the top and bottom borders.

BLACK

- Cut 9 strips 2½" × WOF for double-fold binding.

BACKING

- Cut 3 pieces 32" × 82". Piece them together and trim to about 82" × 95".

tip **Don't try to match your red fabrics too closely; you want a variety of reds. A mix of tomato red, orange red, burgundy red, and so on will give your quilt more interest and a sense of movement.**

INSTRUCTIONS

All seam allowances are ¼". Follow the arrows for pressing suggestions.
For a scrappy look, mix up the fabrics as you sew each block together.

BLOCK ASSEMBLY

Follow the instructions for *Log Jam* Block Assembly (page 46). Make 30.

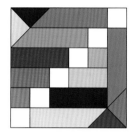

Third in Line block
layout diagram

QUILT CONSTRUCTION

1. Arrange all the blocks into 6 rows of 5 blocks each.

2. Sew together the blocks for each row. Alternate the pressing direction for every other row.

3. Sew together the rows. The quilt top should measure 60½" × 72½".

4. Sew the red 2½" × 72½" inner border strip to each side of the quilt. Press the seam allowance toward the border fabrics.

5. Sew the red 2½" × 64½" inner border strip to the top and bottom of the quilt. Press the seam allowance toward the borders. The quilt top should measure 64½" × 76½".

6. Sew the middle white and outer gray border strips to the quilt top in the same manner as the red inner border strips. The quilt top should measure 75½" × 87½".

QUILTING AND FINISHING

Follow the instructions for *Log Jam* Quilting and Finishing (page 47).

About the Designer

Photo by Jim Colleran

KATE CARLSON COLLERAN made her first quilt for a cousin's baby while she was in college. She's been hooked ever since! A nurse by profession, she often says that quilting is her therapy. In 2003, she launched a quilt pattern company called Seams Like a Dream Quilt Designs with Elizabeth Balderrama. They like to call their design style "traditional with a twist." Together they wrote the book *Smash Your Precut Stash!* (from C&T Publishing). Kate has had her designs published in many quilting magazines. She lives in Colorado. Follow her antics on Seams Like a Dream (seamslikeadream.com).

Starboard

MADE BY MELISSA CORRY

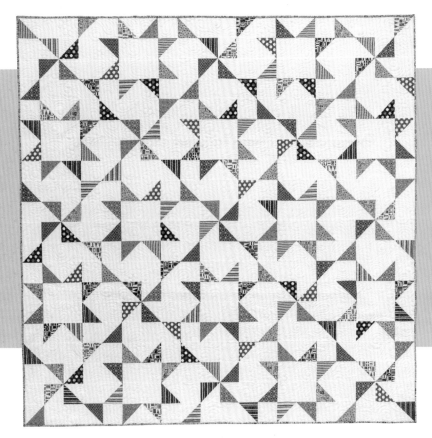

Everyone loves half-square triangles. *Starboard* combines eight half-square triangles with eight squares to create a beautiful twist on a classic design, and the size is perfect to take on a picnic. Each variation tweaks the first quilt. You will still find the same number of triangles and squares in each block, but by using a variety of layouts and a bit of sashing in some, you can make nine different, fabulous quilts.

FINISHED BLOCK SIZE: 16″ × 16″ • **FINISHED QUILT SIZE:** 80½″ × 80½″

MATERIALS

- **Prints:** 13 assorted fat quarters
- **White:** 5¼ yards
- **Binding:** ¾ yard
- **Backing:** 5 yards
- **Batting:** 83″ × 90″

CUTTING

WOF = width of fabric

PRINTS

- Cut 2 strips 5″ × 20″ from each fat quarter.

  Subcut into 8 squares 5″ × 5″. Make a total of 100.

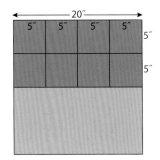

Fat quarter cutting diagram

WHITE

- Cut 13 strips 5″ × WOF.

  Subcut 100 squares 5″ × 5″ for half-square triangle units.

- Cut 25 strips 4½″ × WOF.

  Subcut 200 squares 4½″ × 4½″ for blocks.

BINDING

- Cut 9 strips 2½″ × WOF for double-fold binding.

INSTRUCTIONS

All seam allowances are ¼".

HALF-SQUARE TRIANGLE UNITS

1. Pair 1 white 5" × 5" square and 1 print 5" × 5" square to make half-square triangle units (see Half-Square Triangles, at right). Make 200.

2. Press the seam allowances toward the print fabric. Using the diagonal line on a square ruler matched to the seam on the half-square triangle, trim the half-square units to 4½" × 4½".

BLOCK A

1. Arrange 8 half-square triangle units and 8 white 4½" × 4½" squares as shown.

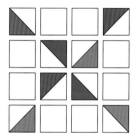

2. Sew the units and squares into rows. Press the seam allowances in opposite directions for every other row.

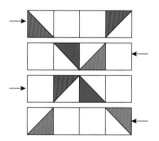

3. Pin and sew together the rows. Press open the seam allowances. Make 13.

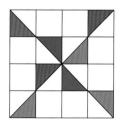

Block A: Make 13.

Half-Square Triangles

1. With right sides together, pair 2 squares. Lightly draw a diagonal line from a corner to the opposite corner on the wrong side of a square.

Draw line.

2. Sew a scant ¼" seam on each side of the line.

Sew.

3. Cut on the drawn line.

4. Press; trim off the dog-ears.

BLOCK B

Follow the instructions for Block A but refer to the Block B diagram for placement of squares and half-square triangles. Make 12.

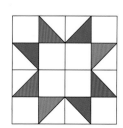

Block B: Make 12.

QUILT CONSTRUCTION

1. Arrange Blocks A and B in 5 rows with 5 blocks per row, alternating the blocks as shown.

Starboard quilt layout

2. Pin and sew the blocks into rows. Press the seams in opposite directions for every other row.

3. Pin and sew together the rows. Press open the seams.

QUILTING AND FINISHING

1. Cut the backing fabric in half to create 2 pieces, each 90″ × WOF. Remove the selvages and sew together the halves using a ½″ seam to create a backing 90″ × 83″. Press the seam to one side.

2. Mark quilting designs on the quilt top or plan to stitch without marking.

3. Layer the backing, batting, and quilt top. Use your preferred method to baste together the 3 layers.

4. Quilt as desired.

5. Bind the quilt.

FINISHED BLOCK SIZE: 16″ × 16″   •   FINISHED QUILT SIZE: 48½″ × 48½″

Blip quilt layout

MATERIALS

- **Prints:** 5 assorted fat quarters
- **White:** 2 yards for background
- **Binding:** ½ yard
- **Backing:** 2¼ yards (assumes 44″-wide fabric)
- **Batting:** 53″ × 53″

CUTTING

WOF = width of fabric

PRINTS

- Cut 2 strips 5″ × 20″ from each fat quarter.

  Subcut 40 squares 5″ × 5″.

WHITE

- Cut 5 strips 5″ × WOF.

  Subcut 40 squares 5″ × 5″ for half-square triangle units.

- Cut 4 strips 4½″ × WOF.

  Subcut 72 squares 4½″ × 4½″ for blocks.

BINDING

- Cut 6 strips 2½″ × WOF for double-fold binding.

INSTRUCTIONS

All seam allowances are ¼".

HALF-SQUARE TRIANGLE UNITS

Follow the instructions for *Starboard* Half-Square Triangle Units (page 55). Make a total of 70 half-square triangle units.

BLOCK

Follow the instructions for *Starboard* Block A (page 55). Make 9 blocks, following the Blip block layout diagram.

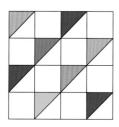

Blip block layout

QUILT CONSTRUCTION

Arrange the blocks in 3 rows with 3 blocks per row, as shown in the *Blip* quilt layout diagram. Follow the instructions for *Starboard* Quilt Construction (page 56).

QUILTING AND FINISHING

1. Remove the selvages from the backing fabric. Cut the backing fabric into a 27" × WOF piece and a 27" × 53" piece. Cut the first piece into 2 rectangles 27" × 22" and sew them together into a long 53" × 22" piece. Press the seam to one side. Sew the first piece and the 53" × 22" piece together using a ½" seam to create a 53" × 63" backing. Press the seam to one side.

2. Follow the instructions for *Starboard* Quilting and Finishing (page 56).

Shattered

FINISHED BLOCK SIZE: 16" × 16" • FINISHED QUILT SIZE: 64½" × 80½"

Shattered quilt layout

MATERIALS

- **Prints:** 10 assorted fat quarters
- **White:** 4¼ yards
- **Binding:** ⅔ yard
- **Backing:** 4 yards (assumes at least 42"-wide fabric)
- **Batting:** 70" × 83"

CUTTING

WOF = width of fabric

PRINTS

- Cut 2 strips 5" × 20" from each fat quarter.

  Subcut 80 squares 5" × 5".

WHITE

- Cut 10 strips 5" × WOF.

  Subcut 80 squares 5" × 5" for half-square triangle units.

- Cut 20 strips 4½" × WOF.

  Subcut 160 squares 4½" × 4½" for blocks.

BINDING

- Cut 8 strips 2½" × WOF for double-fold binding.

INSTRUCTIONS

All seam allowances are ¼".

HALF-SQUARE TRIANGLE UNITS

Follow the instructions for *Starboard* Half-Square Triangle Units (page 55). Make 160 half-square triangle units.

BLOCK

Follow the instructions for *Starboard* Block A (page 55). Use various random layouts for each block, such as those shown. Make 20 blocks.

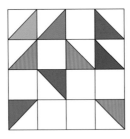 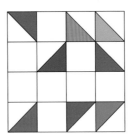

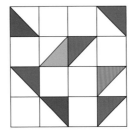

Some Shattered block layout options

QUILT CONSTRUCTION

1. Arrange the blocks in 5 rows with 4 blocks per row, as shown in the *Shattered* quilt layout diagram.

2. Follow the instructions for *Starboard* Quilt Construction (page 56).

QUILTING AND FINISHING

1. Remove the selvages and cut the backing fabric in half to create 2 pieces, each 70" long. Sew the halves together using a ½" seam allowance to create a 70" × 83" backing. Press the seam to one side.

2. Follow the instructions for *Starboard* Quilting and Finishing (page 56).

Crossroads

FINISHED BLOCK SIZE: 16″ × 16″ • **FINISHED QUILT SIZE:** 48½″ × 48½″

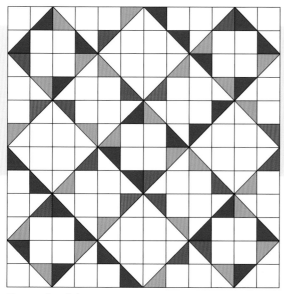
Crossroads quilt layout

MATERIALS

- **Prints:** 5 assorted fat quarters
- **White:** 2 yards
- **Binding:** ½ yard
- **Backing:** 2¼ yards
- **Batting:** 53″ × 53″

CUTTING

WOF = width of fabric

PRINTS

- Cut 2 strips 5″ × 20″ from each fat quarter.

  Subcut 36 squares 5″ × 5″.

WHITE

- Cut 5 strips 5″ × WOF.

  Subcut 36 squares 5″ × 5″ for half-square triangle units.

- Cut 9 strips 4½″ × WOF.

  Subcut 72 squares 4½″ × 4½″ for blocks.

BINDING

- Cut 6 strips 2½″ × WOF for double-fold binding.

INSTRUCTIONS

All seam allowances are ¼″.

HALF-SQUARE TRIANGLE UNITS

Follow the instructions for *Starboard* Half-Square Triangle Units (page 55). Make a total of 72 half-square triangle units.

BLOCK A

Follow the instructions for *Starboard* Block A (page 55). Make 5 blocks using the Crossroads Block A layout diagram.

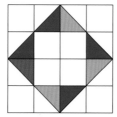
Crossroads Block A layout

BLOCK B

Follow the instructions for *Starboard* Block A (page 55). Make 4 blocks using the Crossroads Block B layout diagram.

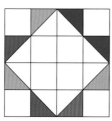
Crossroads Block B layout

QUILT CONSTRUCTION

1. Arrange Blocks A and B in 3 rows with 3 blocks per row, as shown in the *Crossroads* quilt layout diagram.

2. Follow the instructions for *Starboard* Quilt Construction (page 56).

QUILTING AND FINISHING

Follow the instructions for *Blip* Quilting and Finishing (page 57).

Swank

FINISHED BLOCK SIZE: 16″ × 16″ • FINISHED QUILT SIZE: 64½″ × 80½″

Swank quilt layout

MATERIALS

Follow the materials list for *Shattered* (page 57).

CUTTING

Follow the cutting instructions for *Shattered* (page 58).

INSTRUCTIONS

All seam allowances are ¼″.

HALF-SQUARE TRIANGLE UNITS

Follow the instructions for *Starboard* Half-Square Triangle Units (page 55). Make 160 half-square triangle units.

BLOCK A

Follow the instructions for *Starboard* Block A (page 55). Make 10 blocks using the Swank Block A layout diagram.

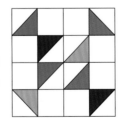

Swank Block A layout

BLOCK B

Follow the instructions for *Starboard* Block A (page 55). Make 10 blocks using the Swank Block B layout diagram.

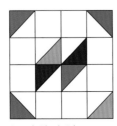

Swank Block B layout

QUILT CONSTRUCTION

1. Arrange Blocks A and B in 5 rows with 4 blocks per row as shown in the *Swank* quilt layout diagram.

2. Follow the instructions for *Starboard* Quilt Construction (page 56).

QUILTING AND FINISHING

1. Remove the selvages. Cut the backing fabric in half to create 2 pieces, each 72″ long. Sew together the halves using a ½″ seam to create a 72″ × 83″ backing. Press the seam to one side.

2. Follow the instructions for *Starboard* Quilting and Finishing (page 56).

Storm in the Desert

FINISHED BLOCK SIZE: 16″ × 16″ • **FINISHED QUILT SIZE: 74½″ × 74½″**

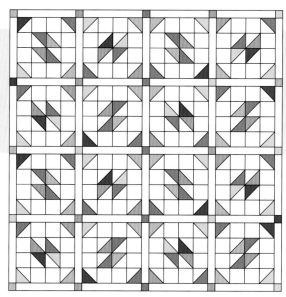

Storm in the Desert quilt layout

INSTRUCTIONS

All seam allowances are ¼″.

HALF-SQUARE TRIANGLE UNITS

Follow the instructions for *Starboard* Half-Square Triangle Units (page 55). Make 128 half-square triangle units.

BLOCK

Follow the instructions for *Starboard* Block A (page 55). Make 16 blocks using the Storm in the Desert block layout diagram.

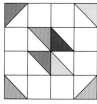

Storm in the Desert block layout

QUILT CONSTRUCTION

1. Arrange the blocks in 4 rows with 4 blocks per row as shown in the *Storm in the Desert* quilt layout diagram.

2. Arrange white 2½″ × 16½″ sashing rectangles and print 2½″ × 2½″ cornerstone squares around the blocks as shown to create the sashing.

MATERIALS

- **Prints:** 8 assorted fat quarters
- **White:** 4¾ yards
- **Binding:** ⅔ yard
- **Backing:** 4⅔ yards
- **Batting:** 83″ × 83″

CUTTING

WOF = width of fabric

PRINTS

- Cut 2 strips 5″ × 20″ from each fat quarter.

  Subcut 64 squares 5″ × 5″. Cut 25 squares 2½″ × 2½″ from the scraps for cornerstones.

WHITE

- Cut 8 strips 5″ × WOF.

  Subcut 64 squares 5″ × 5″ for half-square triangle units.

- Cut 16 strips 4½″ × WOF.

  Subcut 128 squares 4½″ × 4½″ for blocks.

- Cut 20 strips 2½″ × WOF.

  Subcut 40 rectangles 2½″ × 16½″ for sashing.

BINDING

- Cut 8 strips 2½″ × WOF for double-fold binding.

3. Sew the sashing rectangles and cornerstone squares into rows. Press the seams toward the sashing rectangles.

4. Pin and sew the sashing rectangles and blocks into rows. Press the seams toward the sashing rectangles.

5. Pin and sew together the rows. Press open the seams.

QUILTING AND FINISHING

1. Remove the selvages. Cut the backing fabric in half to create 2 pieces, each 83″ × WOF. Sew the halves together using a ½″ seam to create an 83″ × 83″ backing. Press the seam to one side.

2. Follow the instructions for *Starboard* Quilting and Finishing (page 56).

Spinning Star

FINISHED BLOCK SIZE: **16″ × 16″** • FINISHED QUILT SIZE: **67½″ × 84½″**

Spinning Star quilt layout

MATERIALS

- **Prints:** 10 assorted fat quarters
- **White:** 5 yards
- **Binding and cornerstones:** ¾ yard
- **Backing:** 5 yards
- **Batting:** 73″ × 90″

CUTTING

WOF = width of fabric

Follow the cutting instructions for *Shattered* (page 58), except:

WHITE

- Cut 31 rectangles 1½″ × 16½″ for sashing.

CORNERSTONES

- Cut 1 strip 1½″ × WOF.

    Subcut 12 squares 1½″ × 1½″ for cornerstones.

INSTRUCTIONS

All seam allowances are ¼″.

HALF-SQUARE TRIANGLE UNITS

Follow the instructions for *Starboard* Half-Square Triangle Units (page 55). Make 160 half-square triangle units.

BLOCK A

Follow the instructions for *Starboard* Block A (page 55). Make 10 blocks using the Spinning Star Block A layout diagram.

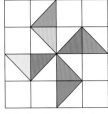

Spinning Star Block A layout

BLOCK B

Follow the instructions for *Starboard* Block A (page 55). Make 10 blocks using the Spinning Star Block B layout diagram.

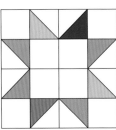

Spinning Star Block B layout

QUILT CONSTRUCTION

1. Arrange the blocks in 5 rows with 4 blocks per row, rotating the blocks as shown in the *Spinning Star* quilt layout diagram.

2. Arrange white 1½" × 16½" rectangles and print 1½" × 1½" squares around the blocks as shown to create the sashing.

3. Sew the sashing rectangles and corner squares into rows. Press the seams toward the sashing rectangles. Pin and sew the sashing rectangles and blocks into rows. Press the seams toward the sashing rectangles.

4. Pin and sew together the rows. Press open the seams.

QUILTING AND FINISHING

1. Remove the selvages. Cut the backing fabric in half to create 2 pieces, each 37" × 90". Sew together the halves using a ½" seam to create a backing 73" × 90". Press the seam to one side.

2. Follow the instructions for *Starboard* Quilting and Finishing (page 56).

O Tannenbaum

FINISHED BLOCK SIZE: **16" × 16"** • FINISHED QUILT SIZE: **91" × 91"**

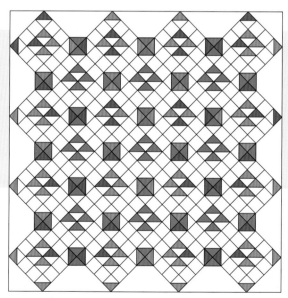

O Tannenbaum **quilt layout**

MATERIALS

- **Red:** 8 assorted fat quarters
- **Green:** 5 assorted fat quarters

- **White:** 7¼ yards
- **Binding:** ⅞ yard
- **Backing:** 8¼ yards
- **Batting:** 99" × 99"

CUTTING

WOF = width of fabric

RED

- Cut 2 strips 5" × 20" from each fat quarter.

  Subcut 64 squares 5" × 5" from the fat quarters.

GREEN

- Cut 2 strips 5" × 20" from each fat quarter.

  Subcut 36 squares 5" × 5" from the fat quarters.

- Cut 12 squares 4½" × 4½" from the scraps for setting triangle blocks.

WHITE

- Cut 13 strips 3″ × WOF.

  Subcut 104 squares 5″ × 5″ for half-square triangle units.

- Cut 25 strips 4½″ × WOF.

  Subcut 200 squares 4½″ × 4½″ for blocks.

- Cut 3 strips 17″ × WOF.

  Subcut 6 squares 17″ × 17″ for setting triangle blocks.

- Cut 1 strip 12¼″ × WOF.

  Subcut 2 squares 12¼″ × 12¼″.

  Subcut diagonally once in half to make 4 corner triangles.

BINDING

- Cut 10 strips 2½″ × WOF for double-fold binding.

INSTRUCTIONS

All seam allowances are ¼″.

HALF-SQUARE TRIANGLE UNITS

Follow the instructions for *Starboard* Half-Square Triangle Units (page 55). Make a total of 208 half-square triangle units: 128 red units and 72 green units.

RED BLOCKS

Follow the instructions for *Starboard* Block A (page 55). Make 16 blocks using the red block layout diagram.

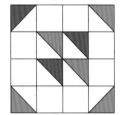

Red block layout

GREEN BLOCKS

Follow the instructions for *Starboard* Block A (page 55). Make 9 blocks using the green block layout diagram.

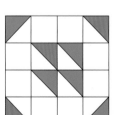

Green block layout

SETTING TRIANGLE BLOCKS

1. Draw a diagonal line on the wrong side of 2 green 4½″ × 4½″ squares. Place the green squares on opposite corners of a white 17″ × 17″ square as shown.

2. Sew directly on each line. Trim away excess fabric ¼″ from the sewn lines. Press the seam allowances toward the green triangles.

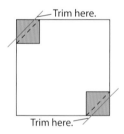

3. Cut the pieced square in half diagonally once to create 2 setting triangle blocks as shown.

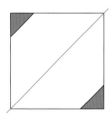

4. Repeat Steps 1–3 to make a total of 12 setting triangle blocks.

Note: Handle bias edges carefully when piecing and pressing.

QUILT CONSTRUCTION

O Tannenbaum assembly diagram

1. Arrange Blocks A and B as shown in the *O Tannenbaum* quilt assembly diagram (at left), adding the setting triangle blocks and corner triangles to complete the quilt top.

2. Pin and sew the blocks into 7 diagonal rows. Press the seams in opposite directions from row to row.

3. Pin and sew together the rows. Press open the seams.

4. Using a rotary cutter and ruler, trim any excess fabric from the setting triangle blocks, leaving ¼″ from the block corners for a seam allowance.

QUILTING AND FINISHING

1. Cut the backing fabric into 3 pieces, each 99″ × WOF. Remove the selvages and sew the pieces together using a ½″ seam. Trim to create a backing 99″ × 99″. Press the seams to one side.

2. Follow the instructions for *Starboard* Quilting and Finishing (page 56).

To Skool

FINISHED BLOCK SIZE: 16″ × 16″ • **FINISHED QUILT SIZE:** 68½″ × 91″

To Skool quilt layout

MATERIALS

- **Prints:** 9 assorted fat quarters
- **White:** 5½ yards
- **Binding:** ⅔ yard
- **Backing:** 5½ yards
- **Batting:** 76″ × 99″

CUTTING

WOF = width of fabric

PRINTS

- Cut 2 strips 5″ × 20″ from each fat quarter.

  Subcut 72 squares 5″ × 5″.

- Cut 6 squares 4½″ × 4½″ from the scraps for vertical setting triangle blocks.

- Cut 4 squares 5″ × 5″ from the scraps.

  Subcut in half diagonally once for horizontal setting triangle blocks.

WHITE

- Cut 9 strips 5" × WOF.

  Subcut 72 squares 5" × 5" for half-square triangle units.

- Cut 18 strips 4½" × WOF.

  Subcut 144 squares 4½" × 4½" for blocks.

- Cut 3 squares 17" × 17" for vertical setting triangle blocks.

- Cut 2 rectangles 9½" × 17" for horizontal setting triangle blocks.

- Cut 4 rectangles 4½" × 13" for horizontal setting triangle blocks.

- Cut 4 squares 5" × 5".

  Subcut in half diagonally once for horizontal setting triangle blocks.

- Cut 2 squares 12¼" × 12¼".

  Subcut in half diagonally once for corner triangles.

BINDING

- Cut 9 strips 2½" × WOF for double-fold binding.

INSTRUCTIONS

All seam allowances are ¼".

HALF-SQUARE TRIANGLE UNITS

Follow the instructions for *Starboard* Half-Square Triangle Units (page 55). Make 144 half-square triangle units.

BLOCK

Follow the instructions for *Starboard* Block A (page 55). Make 18 blocks using the To Skool block layout diagram. Use matching half-square triangles for the fish at the center of each block.

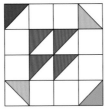

To Skool block layout

> *tip* If you want the corner half-square triangles to match each other, creating a secondary design as in my quilt, follow the *To Skool* quilt layout diagram (page 65) when constructing your blocks.

VERTICAL SETTING TRIANGLE BLOCKS

Follow the instructions for *O Tannenbaum* Setting Triangle Blocks (page 64). Make 6 vertical setting triangle blocks.

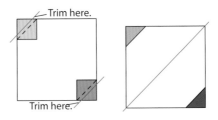

HORIZONTAL SETTING TRIANGLE BLOCKS

1. Make 4 additional half-square triangles by placing together a print triangle and a white triangle, with right sides facing, and sewing along the long edge. Press the seam allowance toward the print fabric and trim the half-square triangle to 4½" × 4½". Make 4.

2. Lay out 2 half-square triangles, 2 white 4½" × 13" rectangles, and 1 white 9" × 17" rectangle as shown. Sew each half-square triangle onto a 4½" × 13" rectangle. Sew these onto opposite sides of the 9" × 17" rectangle to create a 17" × 17" square.

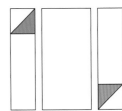

3. Cut the pieced square in half diagonally once to create 2 setting triangle blocks as shown.

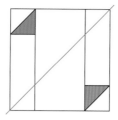

4. Repeat Steps 2 and 3 to make a total of 4 horizontal setting triangle blocks. *Note: Handle bias edges carefully when piecing and pressing.*

QUILT CONSTRUCTION

To Skool quilt assembly

1. Arrange the blocks as shown in the *To Skool* quilt assembly diagram (at left), adding the setting triangle blocks and corner triangles to complete the quilt top layout.

2. Pin and sew the blocks into 6 diagonal rows. Press the seams in opposite directions for every other row.

3. Pin and sew together the rows. Press open the seams.

4. Using a rotary cutter and ruler, trim any excess fabric from the setting triangle blocks, leaving a ¼" seam allowance from the block corners.

QUILTING AND FINISHING

1. Remove the selvages. Cut the backing fabric in half to create 2 pieces, each 99" × WOF. Sew the halves together using a ½" seam allowance to create an 80" × 99" backing. Press the seam to one side.

2. Follow the instructions for *Starboard* Quilting and Finishing (page 56).

About the Designer

MELISSA CORRY started quilting as a hobby in 2005 and now creates tutorials, designs patterns, and blogs about her quilting adventures. She says she is passionate about quilting, loves designing, and finds inspiration in just about everything and anything. Melissa, her husband, and their five little children live in Cedar City, Utah. To learn more about her daily quilting adventures, check out her blog Happy Quilting (www.happyquiltingmelissa.com).

Photo by Kurtis Leany, Zion Photography

Electric

MADE BY TIFFANY JENKINS

When I sat down to design this project, my main goal was to make something fun and edgy for my boys. I initially began with a chevron concept and quickly discovered that with a small flip of the sides, I was able to create an "electric" feeling. As with many simple blocks, an easy turn or a flip can make it take on many different designs!

FINISHED BLOCK SIZE: 10" × 12" • FINISHED QUILT SIZE: 36½" × 40½"

MATERIALS

- **Background:** 1½ yards
- **Accent colors:** 4 fat quarters in different shades
- **Binding:** ½ yard
- **Backing:** 1½ yards
- **Batting:** 42" × 46"
- **Water-soluble fabric marker**

CUTTING

WOF = width of fabric

BACKGROUND

- Cut 9 strips 2½" × WOF.

  Subcut 3 strips into 24 rectangles 2½" × 4½".

  Subcut 2 strips into 24 squares 2½" × 2½".

  Subcut 4 strips into 12 rectangles 2½" × 12½".

- Cut 6 strips 4½" × WOF.

  Subcut 3 strips into 12 rectangles 4½" × 8½".

  Subcut 3 strips into 24 squares 4½" × 4½".

ACCENT COLORS

- Cut pieces from each fat quarter as shown in the fat quarter cutting diagram.

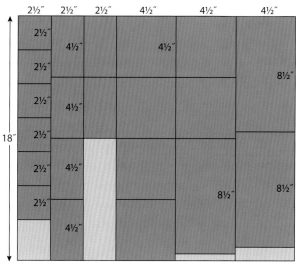

Fat quarter cutting diagram

BINDING

- Cut 5 strips 2½" × WOF for double-fold binding.

Flying Geese

1. Lightly draw a diagonal line from a corner to the opposite corner on the wrong sides of 2 squares.

2. With right sides together, place a square on an end of the rectangle. Sew directly on the line, trim the seam allowance to ¼", and press open.

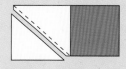

3. With right sides together, place the other square on the other end of the rectangle. Sew directly on the line, trim the seam allowance to ¼", and press open.

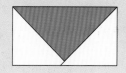

INSTRUCTIONS

All seam allowances are ¼".

BLOCK ASSEMBLY

1. Use the 12 background rectangles 4½" × 8½" and the 24 fat quarter squares 4½" × 4½" to make 12 Flying Geese (see Flying Geese, page 69).

2. Repeat Step 1 with 12 fat quarter rectangles 4½" × 8½" and 24 background squares 4½" × 4½" to make 12 Flying Geese. They will look just like the Flying Geese from Step 1, except the colors will be reversed.

3. Sew together a background rectangle 2½" × 2½" and a fat quarter square 2½" × 2½" along the diagonal of the square, as shown by the dotted line in the Unit A layout diagram. Press open the seam allowance. Make 12, using 3 squares from each fat quarter and 12 background rectangles.

Unit A layout: Make 12.

Trim here.

4. Sew together a background rectangle 2½" × 2½" and a fat quarter square 2½" × 2½" along the diagonal of the square, as shown by the dotted line in the Unit B layout diagram. Press open the seam allowance. Make 12, using 3 squares from each fat quarter and 12 background rectangles.

Unit B layout: Make 12.

Trim here.

5. Sew together 2 Flying Geese, 2 A units, 2 B units, and a background rectangle 2½" × 12½" as shown in the Electric block diagram. Make 3 blocks of each accent color for a total of 12 blocks.

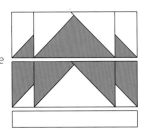

Electric block diagram: Make 12.

QUILT CONSTRUCTION

Arrange the blocks 3 across and 4 down as shown in the *Electric* quilt layout diagram. Keep the same colors in each row, creating a chevron pattern. Sew together the blocks to form rows and then sew together the rows. Press open the seams.

Electric quilt layout

QUILTING AND FINISHING

1. Mark quilting designs on the quilt top or plan to stitch without marking.

2. Layer the backing, batting, and quilt top. Use your preferred method to baste together the 3 layers.

3. Quilt as desired.

4. Bind the quilt.

Shades of Blue

FINISHED BLOCK SIZE: 10″ × 12″ • FINISHED QUILT SIZE: 36½″ × 40″

Shades of Blue quilt layout

In this variation, you can create a different chevron effect simply by flipping Rows 2 and 4 so that they are facing the same direction as Rows 1 and 3. Refer to the *Shades of Blue* quilt layout diagram.

Follow Materials, Cutting, and Block Assembly instructions for *Electric* (page 68).

Stand Out

FINISHED BLOCK SIZE: 10″ × 12″ • FINISHED QUILT SIZE: 53½″ × 45½″

Stand Out quilt layout

MATERIALS

- **Background:** 2 yards (for 15 squares)
- **Accent colors:** 5 different fat quarters
- **Stand Out block:** 1 fat quarter
- **Sashing:** 1 yard (also used for Stand Out block background)
- **Binding:** ½ yard
- **Backing:** 2⅞ yards
- **Batting:** 60″ × 52″

CUTTING

WOF = width of fabric

ACCENT COLORS

- Cut 5 fat quarters as shown in the *Electric* fat quarter cutting diagram (page 69). Each fat quarter will make 3 blocks. Save the Stand Out block fat quarter to cut out later.

BACKGROUND

Follow the cutting instructions for *Electric* (page 69).

SASHING

- Cut 14 strips 1½" × WOF.

  Subcut 4 of the strips into 12 rectangles 1½" × 10½".

  Sew together 7 strips (end to end). Subcut into 5 rectangles 1½" × 52½".

  Sew together 3 strips (end to end). Subcut into 2 rectangles 1½" × 45½".

STAND OUT BLOCK:

Cut both the Stand Out fat quarter and the remaining sashing fabric:

- Cut 1 rectangle 4½" × 8½".

- Cut 2 squares 4½" × 4½".

- Cut 2 rectangles 2½" × 4½".

- Cut 2 squares 2½" × 2½".

- Cut 1 strip 2½" × 12½".

BINDING

- Cut 6 strips 2½" × WOF for double-fold binding.

INSTRUCTIONS

BLOCK ASSEMBLY

Follow the instructions for *Electric* Block Assembly (page 70). Assembly for the Stand Out block is the same as for the rest of the blocks. Make 16 blocks.

QUILT CONSTRUCTION

1. Place the blocks in 4 rows of 4 blocks each.

2. Sew a 1½" × 10½" sashing strip between the blocks across each row.

3. Sew a 1½" × 52½" sashing strip between the rows and at the top and bottom of the quilt.

4. Sew the remaining 2 strips 1½" × 45½" along each long edge of the quilt.

5. Follow the instructions for *Electric* Quilting and Finishing (page 70).

Magnetic

FINISHED BLOCK SIZE: 8″ × 12″ • FINISHED QUILT SIZE: 32½″ × 36½″

Magnetic quilt layout

INSTRUCTIONS

BLOCK ASSEMBLY

1. Follow the instructions for *Electric* Block Assembly (page 70). Make 6 blocks from the fat quarters using dark gray for 3 backgrounds and light gray for the other 3 backgrounds.

2. Instead of adding 2½″ × 12½″ strips to the bottom of the blocks as shown in the Electric block diagram, sew a *matching* 8½″ × 12½″ rectangle to the bottom of each square.

QUILT CONSTRUCTION

1. Arrange the blocks with the point in the first and third row facing inward and the point in the second row facing outward. Sew together the blocks in 2 rows of 3 blocks and then sew together the rows as shown in the *Magnetic* quilt layout diagram.

2. Follow the instructions for *Electric* Quilting and Finishing (page 70).

MATERIALS

- **Fat quarters:** 3 different colors
- **Dark gray:** 1 yard
- **Light gray:** 1 yard
- **Binding:** ⅓ yard
- **Batting:** 38″ × 42″
- **Backing:** 1¼ yards

CUTTING

FAT QUARTERS

From *each*:

- Cut 4 squares 2½″ × 2½″.
- Cut 4 rectangles 2½″ × 4½″.
- Cut 4 squares 4½″ × 4½″.
- Cut 2 rectangles 4½″ × 8½″.

BACKGROUND

From *each* gray color:

- Cut 1 strip 8½″ × WOF.

  Subcut 3 rectangles 8½″ × 12½″.

- Cut 3 strips 4½″ × WOF.

  Subcut 3 rectangles 4½″ × 8½″.

  Subcut 6 squares 4½″ × 4½″.

- Cut 2 strips 2½″ × WOF.

  Subcut 6 rectangles 2½″ × 4½″.

  Subcut 6 squares 2½″ × 2½″.

BINDING

- Cut 4 strips 2½″ × WOF for double-fold binding.

Keystones

FINISHED BLOCK SIZE: **14″ × 14″** • FINISHED QUILT SIZE: **42½″ × 56½″**

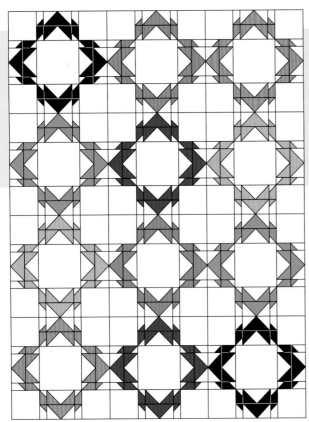

Keystones **quilt layout**

MATERIALS

- **Accent colors:** 6 fat quarters
- **White:** 2½ yards
- **Binding:** 1⅛ yards
- **Batting:** 48″ × 62″
- **Backing:** 2½ yards
- **Batting:** 2 pieces 70″ × 82″

CUTTING

WOF = width of fabric

FAT QUARTERS

Each fat quarter will make 2 quilt blocks. Keep colors separate.

From *each*:

- Cut 8 rectangles 2½″ × 4½″.
- Cut 16 squares 2½″ × 2½″.
- Cut 16 squares 1½″ × 1½″.
- Cut 16 rectangles 1½″ × 2½″.

WHITE

- Cut 6 strips 4½″ × WOF.

  Subcut into 48 squares 4½″ × 4½″.

- Cut 2 strips 6½″ × WOF.

  Subcut into 12 squares 6½″ × 6½″.

- Cut 12 strips 2½″ × WOF.

  Subcut 6 strips into 48 rectangles 2½″ × 4½″.

  Subcut 6 strips into 96 squares 2½″ × 2½″.

- Cut 10 strips 1½″ × WOF.

  Subcut 4 strips into 96 squares 1½″ × 1½″.

  Subcut 6 strips into 96 rectangles 1½″ × 2½″.

BINDING

- Cut 6 strips 2½″ × WOF for double-fold binding.

BLOCK ASSEMBLY

Each block will need the following:

4 white squares 4½″ × 4½″	4 colored rectangles 2½″ × 4½″
1 white square 6½″ × 6½″	8 colored squares 2½″ × 2½″
4 white rectangles 2½″ × 4½″	8 colored squares 1½″ × 1½″
8 white squares 2½″ × 2½″	8 colored rectangles 1½″ × 2½″
8 white squares 1½″ × 1½″	
8 white rectangles 1½″ × 2½″	

1. Using the 4 white rectangles 2½″ × 4½″ and the 8 colored squares 2½″ × 2½″, make 4 of the Flying Geese (see Flying Geese, page 69).

2. Repeat Step 1, using the 4 colored rectangles 2½″ × 4½″ and the 8 white squares 2½″ × 2½″ make 4 Flying Geese.

3. Using the 8 white rectangles 1½″ × 2½″ and the 8 colored squares 1½″ × 1½″, make 4 of the units shown in the *Electric* Unit A layout diagram (page 70). Make 4 of the units shown in the *Electric* Unit B layout diagram (page 70).

4. Repeat Step 3, using the 8 colored rectangles 1½″ × 2½″ and the 8 white squares 1½″ × 1½″ to make 4 A units and 4 B units.

5. Sew together the units as shown in the Electric block diagram (page 70). There will NOT be a strip across the bottom as shown in the diagram. Make 4.

6. Assemble the 4 units created in Step 5, the 4 white squares 4½″ × 4½″, and the white square 6½″ × 6½″ as shown in the Keystone block layout diagram. Make 12 blocks.

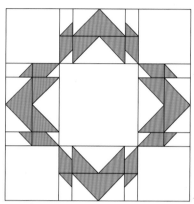

Keystone block layout

QUILT CONSTRUCTION

1. Arrange the blocks in 2 rows of 3 blocks. Sew together the rows as shown in the *Keystones* quilt layout diagram (page 74).

2. Follow the instructions for *Electric* Quilting and Finishing (page 70).

About the Designer

Photo by Kristen Pack

TIFFANY JENKINS loves traditional quilt blocks but always tries to push herself to create something that hasn't been seen before. Her business, Tiny Seamstress, started as a blog where she showed off pictures of bags she was sewing. Named in honor of her height (4′8¾″), the design company now also sells patterns for bags and quilts. She loves that quilting presents her with a challenge "to take something old and make it new again."

Kim's Deal

MADE BY JO KRAMER AND KELLI HANKEN

As designers we love taking the old traditional blocks and sprucing them up into a more modern design. What is more classic than the Churn Dash block? Best yet, it's simple to construct and offers loads of variations. We took the block, turned it on point, and then let the color placement and border treatments take that classic block into a modern-day quilt that is perfect for gift giving or keeping for you.

FINISHED BLOCK SIZE: 10″ × 10″ • FINISHED QUILT SIZE: 69″ × 69″

MATERIALS

- **Colored:** 14 fat quarters
- **Neutral:** 4 fat quarters
- **Dark print:** 3½ yards (binding included)
- **Backing:** 4¼ yards
- **Batting:** 74½″ × 74½″

CUTTING

WOF = width of fabric

COLORED FAT QUARTERS

- Cut 25 matching sets of 2 squares 4⅞″ × 4⅞″ (50 total).

- Cut 241 squares 2½″ × 2½″. Select 25 matching sets of 4 squares 2½″ × 2½″ for the blocks. The rest will be used in the border.

NEUTRAL FAT QUARTERS

- Cut 9 sets of 2 squares 4⅞″ × 4⅞″ (18 total).

- Cut 9 sets of 4 squares 2½″ × 2½″ (36 total).

DARK PRINT

- Cut 4 strips 4⅞″ × WOF.

  Subcut into 32 squares 4⅞″ × 4⅞″.

- Cut 12 strips 2½″ × WOF.

  Subcut 4 strips into 64 squares 2½″ × 2½″.

  The remaining 8 strips 2½″ × WOF will be used for binding.

- Cut 2 strips 15⅜″ × WOF.

  Subcut into 3 squares 15⅜″ × 15⅜″ and cut each square twice diagonally.

- Cut 1 strip 8″ × WOF.

  Subcut into 2 squares 8″ × 8″ and cut each square once diagonally.

- Cut 7 strips 4½″ × WOF for the outer border.

Churn Dash Block

All of the quilts in this chapter include Churn Dash blocks. Refer to these instructions for all of the designs.

MATERIALS

- **Unit A:** 2 background squares 4⅞″ × 4⅞″ and 2 colored squares 4⅞″ × 4⅞″

- **Unit B:** 4 background squares 2½″ × 2½″

- **Unit C:** 4 colored squares 2½″ × 2½″

- **Unit D:** 1 coordinating square 2½″ × 2½″

- **Fabric marker, pencil, or chalk**

1. Pair a colored square 4⅞″ × 4⅞″ with a background square 4⅞″ × 4⅞″. Make 4 half-square triangles (see Half-Square Triangles, page 55), pressing the seam toward the darker triangle (A).

2. Sew an outer colored square 2½″ × 2½″ (B) to an inner colored square 2½″ × 2½″ (C) to make a connector (B/C). Make 4.

3. Make an outer row by sewing a half-square triangle (A) to a connector (B/C), noting the position of the inner and outer squares. Sew a second half-square triangle to the connector. Press toward the connector. Make 2.

4. Make the center row by sewing a connector (B/C) to the center square (D). Sew the final connector to the opposite side of the center square. Press toward the connectors. Make 1.

5. To complete the block, sew 2 outer rows to the center row. Press.

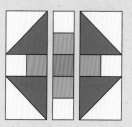

Churn Dash block construction

INSTRUCTIONS

All seam allowances are ¼".

BLOCK ASSEMBLY

To construct the blocks, refer to Churn Dash Block (page 77).

Follow the block layout diagrams and chart (below and at right) to group your squares into sets before constructing the Churn Dash blocks. Use a variety of colors for the different blocks, but select matching colors and neutrals for each block.

	4⅞" × 4⅞" squares	2½" × 2½" squares	Number to make
LIGHT BLOCK	2 colored 2 neutral	4 colored 4 neutral 1 coordinating color	9 light blocks
DARK BLOCK	2 colored 2 dark	4 colored 4 dark 1 coordinating color	16 dark blocks

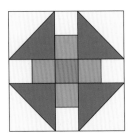

Light block layout

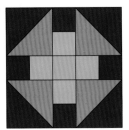

Dark block layout

QUILT CONSTRUCTION

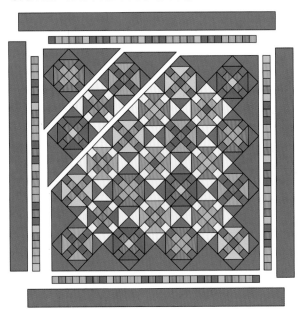

Kim's Deal quilt layout

1. Assemble the quilt center, alternating light and dark blocks. Attach setting triangles to the end of each row. Assemble rows to complete the quilt center.

2. Sew together 28 squares 2½" × 2½", using a scant ¼" seam. Press seams. Make 2.

3. Sew together 30 squares 2½" × 2½", using a scant ¼" seam. Press seams. Make 2.

4. Attach each shorter border to the sides of the quilt. Press toward the pieced border.

5. Attach each longer border to the top and bottom of the quilt. Press toward the pieced border.

6. Piece together the 7 border strips 4½" × WOF. Measure your quilt vertically through the center. Cut 2 border strips to this measurement. Attach a border to each side of the quilt. Press toward the border.

7. Measure your quilt horizontally through the center. Cut 2 border strips to this measurement. Attach to the top and bottom of the quilt. Press toward the border.

QUILTING AND FINISHING

1. Mark quilting designs on the quilt top or plan to stitch without marking.

2. Layer the backing, batting, and quilt top. Use your preferred method to baste together the 3 layers.

3. Quilt as desired.

4. Bind the quilt.

Coral Reef

FINISHED BLOCK SIZE: 10" × 10" • FINISHED QUILT SIZE: 80½" × 80½"

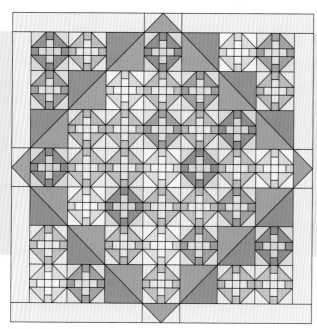

Coral Reef quilt layout

MATERIALS

- **Pink, teal, orange, green, and yellow:** 2 fat quarters of each
- **Light pink, light teal, light orange, light green, and light yellow:** 2 fat quarters of each
- **Green print:** 1¼ yards
- **Teal print:** 1⅝ yards (binding included)
- **Neutral print:** 1¾ yards (for the border)
- **Batting:** 88" × 88"
- **Backing:** 7 yards

CUTTING

WOF = width of fabric

PINK, ORANGE, LIGHT PINK, AND LIGHT ORANGE

From each color:

- Cut 8 sets of 2 squares 4⅞" × 4⅞" (16 total of each color).
- Cut 8 sets of 4 squares 2½" × 2½" (32 total of each color).

TEAL, GREEN, YELLOW, LIGHT TEAL, LIGHT GREEN, AND LIGHT YELLOW

From each color:

- Cut 7 sets of 2 squares 4⅞" × 4⅞" (14 total of each color).

- Cut 7 sets of 4 squares 2½" × 2½" (28 total of each color).

NEUTRAL

- Cut 10 strips 5½" × WOF.

  Subcut 2 strips into 8 squares 5½" × 5½".

  Subcut 4 strips into 4 rectangles 5½" × 30½".

  Subcut 4 strips into 4 rectangles 5½" × 35½".

GREEN PRINT

- Cut 3 strips 10⅞" × WOF.

  Subcut 6 squares 10⅞" × 10⅞".

- Cut 1 strip 5½" × WOF.

  Subcut 4 rectangles 5½" × 10".

TEAL PRINT

- Cut 3 strips 10⅞" × WOF.

  Subcut 6 squares 10⅞" × 10⅞".

- Cut 9 strips 2½" × WOF for double-fold binding.

INSTRUCTIONS

All seam allowances are ¼".

BLOCK ASSEMBLY

To construct the blocks, refer to Churn Dash Block (page 77).

1. Follow the block layout diagrams and chart below to group your squares into sets before constructing the Churn Dash blocks. Use a variety of colors for the different blocks, but select matching colors and neutrals for each block.

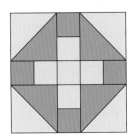

Coral Reef block layout

	4⅞" × 4⅞" squares	2½" × 2½" squares	Number to make
CHURN DASH BLOCK	2 colored 2 coordinating light color	4 colored 5 coordinating light color	8 pink 8 orange 7 teal 7 green 7 yellow

2. Pair a teal square 10⅞" × 10⅞" with a green square 10⅞" × 10⅞". Make 12 half-square triangle units (see Half-Square Triangles, page 55).

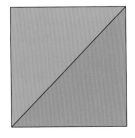

Teal and green half-square triangles

QUILT CONSTRUCTION

1. Arrange the teal and green half-square triangles and the Churn Dash blocks to create the quilt center. Sew together the blocks in rows and then sew together the rows.

2. Pair 2 neutral squares 5½" × 5½" with a green rectangle 5½" × 10½". Make 4 Flying Geese units (see Flying Geese, page 69).

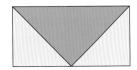

Flying Geese unit

3. Sew a neutral strip 5½" × 30½" to each side of a green-and-neutral Flying Geese unit. Press toward the neutral strip. Make 2. Attach this strip to the sides of the quilt, taking care to center the Flying Geese unit.

4. Sew a neutral strip 5½" × 35½" to each side of the remaining Flying Geese unit. Press toward the neutral strip. Make 2. Attach this strip to the top and bottom of the quilt, taking care to center the Flying Geese unit.

QUILTING AND FINISHING

Follow the instructions for *Kim's Deal* Quilting and Finishing (page 79).

Miss Molly

FINISHED BLOCK SIZE: **10" × 10"** • FINISHED QUILT SIZE: **57" × 57"**

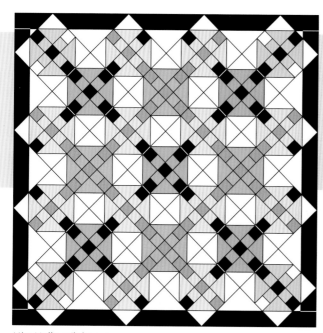

Miss Molly **quilt layout**

MATERIALS

- **Pink:** 7 fat quarters
- **Black:** 2 yards (binding included)
- **Gray:** ½ yard
- **White:** 1⅔ yards
- **Batting:** 62" × 62"
- **Backing:** 3½ yards

CUTTING

WOF = width of fabric

PINK

- Cut 25 sets of 2 squares 4⅞" × 4⅞" (50 total).
- Cut 25 sets of 4 squares 2½" × 2½" (100 total).

BLACK

- Cut 11 strips 2½" × WOF.

  Subcut 4 strips into 61 squares 2½" × 2½".

  The remaining 7 strips will be used for double-fold binding.

- Cut 8 strips 3⅜" × WOF.

  Subcut 6 strips into 12 rectangles 3⅜" × 18".

  Subcut 1 strip into 4 rectangles 3⅜" × 6".

  Subcut 1 strip into 4 rectangles 3⅜" × 9".

INSTRUCTIONS

All seam allowances are ¼".

GRAY

- Cut 4 strips 2½" × WOF.

  Subcut into 56 squares 2½" × 2½".

WHITE

- Cut 7 strips 4⅞" × WOF.

  Subcut into 50 squares 4⅞" × 4⅞".

- Cut 1 strip 2½" × WOF.

  Subcut into 8 squares 2½" × 2½".

- Cut 1 strip 9¾" × WOF.

  Subcut into 3 squares 9¾" × 9¾".
  Then cut each square twice on
  the diagonal.

- Cut 1 strip 2⅜" × WOF.

  Subcut into 2 squares 2⅜" × 2⅜".
  Then cut each square once on
  the diagonal.

BLOCK ASSEMBLY

To construct the blocks, refer to Churn Dash Block (page 77).

1. Follow the block layout diagrams and chart below to group your fabrics into sets before constructing the Churn Dash blocks. Use a variety of pinks for each block, but select matching pinks for each block.

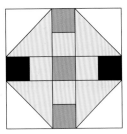

Block A layout

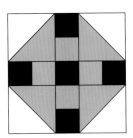

Block B layout

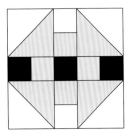

Block C layout

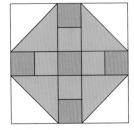

Block D layout

	4⅞" × 4⅞" squares	2½" × 2½" squares	Number to make
BLOCK A	2 pink 2 white	4 pink 3 gray 2 black	12
BLOCK B	2 pink 2 white	4 pink 5 black	5
BLOCK C	2 pink 2 white	4 pink 2 white 3 black	4
BLOCK D	2 pink 2 white	4 pink 5 gray	4

2. Along the long side, fold in half each of the triangles that were cut from the 9¾″ × 9¾″ squares. Place a pin here. Fold a 3⅜″ × 18″ rectangle in half and pin in the middle. With right sides together, match up the pins and sew the white triangle to the black rectangle. Press toward the black rectangle. Use a ruler to extend the edges of the setting triangle; trim with a rotary cutter. Make 12.

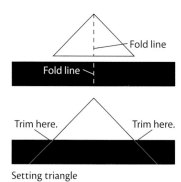

Setting triangle

3. To make the pieced corner setting triangles, sew a black rectangle 3⅜″ × 6″ to a triangle cut from the 2⅜″ × 2⅜″ square. Press toward the black. Make 4.

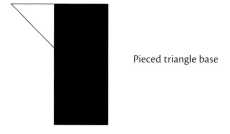

Pieced triangle base

4. Attach a black 3⅜″ × 9″ rectangle to the triangle base. Press toward the black. Repeat for each base. Make 4.

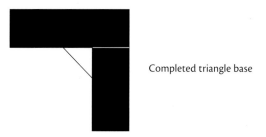

Completed triangle base

5. Mark each side 8″ from the corner and use a ruler to trim the triangle base. After trimming, each black side of the triangle should measure 8″. Repeat for each triangle base. Make 4 corner setting triangles.

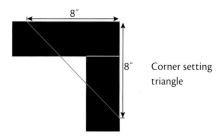

Corner setting triangle

QUILT CONSTRUCTION

Refer as needed to the instructions for Kim's Deal *Quilt Construction (page 78).*

Assemble the quilt as shown in the *Miss Molly* quilt layout diagram (page 81). Use the pieced blocks, pieced setting triangles, and corner setting triangles.

QUILTING AND FINISHING

Follow the instructions for *Kim's Deal* Quilting and Finishing (page 79).

Ruby Red

FINISHED BLOCK SIZE: 10″ × 10″ • FINISHED QUILT SIZE: 57″ × 57″

Ruby Red quilt layout

MATERIALS

- **Red prints:** 3 fat quarters
- **Red-and-white print:** 1 fat quarter
- **White print:** 3 fat quarters
- **Dark gray:** 1⅞ yards
- **Medium gray:** ¾ yard
- **Light gray:** ¾ yard
- **Black:** ⅝ yard for binding
- **Batting:** 62″ × 62″
- **Backing:** 3⅔ yards

CUTTING

WOF = width of fabric

RED

- Cut 9 sets of 2 squares 4⅞″ × 4⅞″ (18 total).
- Cut 9 sets of 4 squares 2½″ × 2½″ (36 total).

RED-AND-WHITE PRINT

- Cut 4 sets of 2 squares 4⅞″ × 4⅞″ (8 total).
- Cut 4 sets of 4 squares 2½″ × 2½″ (16 total).

WHITE PRINT

- Cut 12 sets of 2 squares 4⅞″ × 4⅞″ (24 total).
- Cut 12 sets of 4 squares 2½″ × 2½″ (48 total).

DARK GRAY

- Cut 2 strips 4⅞″ × WOF.

  Subcut into 14 squares 4⅞″ × 4⅞″.
- Cut 4 strips 2½″ × WOF.

  Subcut into 49 squares 2½″ × 2½″.
- Cut 2 strips 15½″ × WOF.

  Subcut into 3 squares 15½″ × 15½″. Cut each square twice diagonally for setting triangles.
- Cut 1 strip 8″ × WOF.

  Subcut into 2 squares 8″ × 8″. Cut each square once diagonally for corner triangles.

MEDIUM GRAY

- Cut 2 strips 4⅞″ × WOF.

  Subcut into 26 squares 4⅞″ × 4⅞″.
- Cut 4 strips 2½″ × WOF.

  Subcut into 56 squares 2½″ × 2½″.

LIGHT GRAY

- Cut 1 strip 4⅞″ × WOF.

  Subcut into 8 squares 4⅞″ × 4⅞″.
- Cut 2 strips 2½″ × WOF.

  Subcut into 20 squares 2½″ × 2½″.

BLACK

- Cut 7 strips 2½″ × WOF for double-fold binding.

INSTRUCTIONS

All seam allowances are ¼".

BLOCK ASSEMBLY

To construct the blocks, refer to Churn Dash Block (page 77).

Follow the assembly diagrams and chart below to group your fabrics into sets before constructing the Churn Dash blocks. Use a variety of reds and grays for the different blocks, but select matching colors for each block.

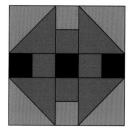

Block A layout

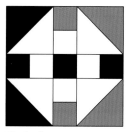

Block B layout

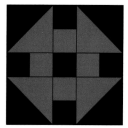

Block C layout

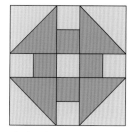

Block D layout

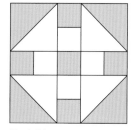

Block E layout

QUILT CONSTRUCTION

Refer as needed to the instructions for Kim's Deal *Quilt Construction (page 78).*

Assemble the quilt as shown in the *Ruby Red* quilt layout diagram (page 84). Pay special attention to the placement of the center blocks so that they form a star. Add the remaining blocks, setting triangles, and corner triangles. Sew the blocks into rows and then sew the rows to create the quilt top.

QUILTING AND FINISHING

Follow the instructions for *Kim's Deal* Quilting and Finishing (page 79).

	4⅞" × 4⅞" squares	2½" × 2½" squares	Number to make
BLOCK A	2 red 2 medium gray	4 red 2 medium gray 3 dark gray	4
BLOCK B	2 white print 1 medium gray 1 dark gray	4 white print 2 medium gray 3 dark gray	4
BLOCK C	2 red 2 dark gray	4 red 5 dark gray	5
BLOCK D	2 red-and-white print 2 light gray	4 red-and-white print 5 light gray	4
BLOCK E	2 white print 2 medium gray	4 white print 5 medium gray	8

Star Gazer

FINISHED BLOCK SIZE: 10″ × 10″ • **FINISHED QUILT SIZE: 71″ × 71″**

Star Gazer quilt layout

MATERIALS

- **White print:** 3 fat quarters
- **Turquoise, pink, green, yellow, and orange solids:** 1 fat quarter of each
- **Pink and green prints:** 2 fat quarters of each
- **Turquoise, yellow, and orange prints:** 1 fat quarter of each
- **Charcoal solid:** 3½ yards
- **Black solid:** 1⅛ yards (binding included)
- **Batting:** 78″ × 78″
- **Backing:** 4⅓″ yards

CUTTING

WOF = width of fabric

WHITE PRINT

- Cut 25 sets of 4 squares 2½″ × 2½″ (100 total).

PINK SOLID

- Cut 4 squares 4⅞″ × 4⅞″.
- Cut 7 squares 2½″ × 2½″.

TURQUOISE SOLID

- Cut 4 squares 4⅞″ × 4⅞″.
- Cut 4 squares 2½″ × 2½″.

GREEN SOLID

- Cut 4 squares 4⅞″ × 4⅞″.
- Cut 5 squares 2½″ × 2½″.

YELLOW SOLID

- Cut 2 squares 4⅞″ × 4⅞″.
- Cut 8 squares 2½″ × 2½″.

ORANGE SOLID

- Cut 2 squares 4⅞″ × 4⅞″.
- Cut 4 squares 2½″ × 2½″.

PINK PRINT

- Cut 7 sets of 2 squares 4⅞″ × 4⅞″ (14 total).
- Cut 7 sets of 4 squares 2½″ × 2½″ (28 total).

GREEN PRINT

- Cut 5 sets of 2 squares 4⅞″ × 4⅞″ (10 total).
- Cut 5 sets of 4 squares 2½″ × 2½″ (20 total).

TURQUOISE PRINT

- Cut 8 squares 4⅞″ × 4⅞″.
- Cut 16 squares 2½″ × 2½″.

YELLOW PRINT

- Cut 8 squares 4⅞″ × 4⅞″.
- Cut 16 squares 2½″ × 2½″.

ORANGE PRINT

- Cut 8 squares 4⅞″ × 4⅞″.
- Cut 16 squares 2½″ × 2½″.

CHARCOAL SOLID

- Cut 4 strips 4⅞″ × WOF.

  Subcut into 32 squares 4⅞″ × 4⅞″.

- Cut 9 strips 4½″ × WOF.

  Subcut 1 strip into 4 squares 4½″ × 4½″.

  The remaining strips will be used for the outer border.

CHARCOAL SOLID, CONTINUED

- Cut 6 strips 2½" × WOF for the inner border.

- Cut 2 strips 15½" × WOF.

  Subcut into 3 squares 15½" × 15½". Cut twice diagonally to yield 12 triangles.

- Cut 1 strip 8" × WOF.

  Subcut into 2 squares 8" × 8". Cut once diagonally to yield 4 triangles.

BLACK SOLID

- Cut 7 strips 1½" × WOF for middle border.

- Cut 8 strips 2½" × WOF for double-fold binding.

INSTRUCTIONS

All seam allowances are ¼".

BLOCK ASSEMBLY

To construct the blocks, refer to Churn Dash Block (page 77).

Follow the assembly diagrams (below) and chart (at right) to group your fabrics into sets before constructing the Churn Dash blocks. Use a variety of colors for the different blocks, but select matching colors for each block. *Note: The center block uses 4½" × 4½" squares instead of half-square triangles in the 4 corners of the block.*

	4⅞" × 4⅞" squares	2½" × 2½" squares	Number to make
BLOCK A	2 solid colors 2 matching prints	4 matching prints 4 white prints 1 solid color	2 pink 2 turquoise 2 green 1 yellow 1 orange
BLOCK B	2 matching prints 2 charcoal solids	4 matching prints 4 white prints 1 solid color	5 pink 3 green 3 yellow 3 orange 2 turquoise
CENTER BLOCK	4 charcoal squares 4½" × 4½"	4 yellow 4 white prints 1 charcoal solid	1 yellow

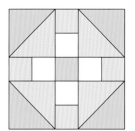

Block A layout

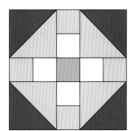

Block B layout

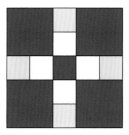

Center block layout

QUILT CONSTRUCTION

Refer as needed to the instructions for Kim's Deal *Quilt Construction (page 78).*

1. Assemble the quilt as shown in the *Star Gazer* quilt layout diagram (page 86). Use the setting triangles, corner triangles, and pieced blocks.

2. To construct the inner border, piece the 6 strips 2½" × WOF on the diagonal. Measure your quilt vertically through the middle. Cut 2 borders to this measurement. Attach the borders to the opposite sides of the quilt. Press the seam allowances toward the border.

3. Measure your quilt horizontally through the middle. Cut 2 segments to this measurement. Attach the borders to the top and bottom of the quilt. Press the seam allowances toward the border.

4. To construct the middle border, piece the 7 strips 1½″ × WOF on the diagonal. Measure your quilt vertically through the middle. Cut 2 borders to this measurement. Attach the borders to opposite sides of the quilt. Press the seam allowances toward the border.

5. Measure your quilt horizontally through the middle. Cut 2 borders to this measurement. Attach the borders to the top and bottom of the quilt. Press the seam allowances toward the border.

6. For the outer border, piece the 8 strips 4½″ × WOF on the diagonal. Measure your quilt vertically through the middle. Cut 2 segments to this measurement. Attach the strips to opposite sides of the quilt. Press toward the border.

7. Measure your quilt horizontally through the middle. Cut 2 segments to this measurement. Attach to the top and bottom of the quilt. Press toward the border.

QUILTING AND FINISHING

Follow instructions for *Kim's Deal* Quilting and Finishing (page 79).

Tell Me a Secret

FINISHED BLOCK SIZE: **10″ × 10″** • FINISHED QUILT SIZE: **57″ × 57″**

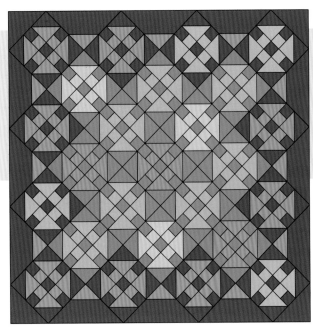

Tell Me a Secret quilt layout

MATERIALS

- **Pink:** 8 fat quarters
- **Turquoise:** 1⅝ yards (binding included)
- **Brown:** 2 yards
- **Batting:** 65″ × 65″
- **Backing:** 3⅔ yards

CUTTING

WOF = width of fabric

PINK

- Cut 25 sets of 2 squares 4⅞″ × 4⅞″ (50 total).
- Cut 25 sets of 4 squares 2½″ × 2½″ (100 total).
- Cut 12 squares 4½″ × 4½″.

TURQUOISE

- Cut 4 strips 4⅞″ × WOF.

  Subcut into 26 squares 4⅞″ × 4⅞″.

- Cut 12 strips 2½″ × WOF.

  Subcut into 65 squares 2½″ × 2½″.

  The remaining 7 strips 2½″ × WOF will be used for double-fold binding.

BROWN

- Cut 3 strips 4⅞" × WOF.

  Subcut into 24 squares 4⅞" × 4⅞".

- Cut 4 strips 2½" × WOF.

  Subcut into 60 squares 2½" × 2½".

- Cut 2 strips 15½" × WOF.

  Subcut into 3 squares 15½" × 15½". Cut each square twice diagonally.

- Cut 1 strip 8" × WOF.

  Subcut into 2 squares 8" × 8". Cut each once diagonally.

INSTRUCTIONS

All seam allowances are ¼".

BLOCK ASSEMBLY

To construct the blocks, refer to Churn Dash Block (page 77).

Follow the assembly diagrams and chart below to group your fabrics into sets before constructing the Churn Dash blocks. Use a variety of pinks for the different blocks, but select matching pinks for each block. Make 13 A blocks and 12 B blocks.

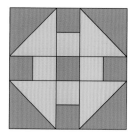
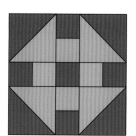

Block A layout   Block B layout

	4⅞" × 4⅞" squares	2½" × 2½" squares	Number to make
BLOCK A	2 pink 2 turquoise	4 pink 5 turquoise	13
BLOCK B	2 pink 2 brown	4 pink 5 brown	12

QUILT CONSTRUCTION

1. Draw a line on the back of each pink 4½" × 4½" square, connecting opposite corners.

2. With right sides together, place a pink square on the right angle side of each setting triangle. Sew on the drawn line. Trim the outer seam to ¼". Press toward the pink fabric. Make 12.

Tell Me a Secret setting triangles

3. Arrange your quilt as shown in the *Tell Me a Secret* quilt layout diagram (page 88). Place turquoise blocks in the center of the quilt, with the brown blocks around the turquoise center. Add the pieced setting triangles around the edges of the quilt and place the corner setting triangles in each corner. Sew together the quilt first in rows and then sew together the rows.

QUILTING AND FINISHING

Follow the instructions for *Kim's Deal* Quilting and Finishing (page 79).

X Marks the Spot

FINISHED BLOCK SIZE: 10″ × 10″ • FINISHED QUILT SIZE: 57″ × 57″

X Marks the Spot quilt layout

MATERIALS

- **Pink:** 2 fat quarters
- **Green:** 2 fat quarters
- **Turquoise:** 1 fat quarter
- **Yellow:** 1 fat quarter
- **Orange:** 1 fat quarter
- **White print:** 1 fat quarter

- **Dark turquoise:** 1½ yards (binding included)
- **Medium turquoise:** ¾ yard
- **Light turquoise:** 1 yard
- **White:** ½ yard
- **Batting:** 65″ × 65″
- **Backing:** 3⅔ yards

CUTTING

WOF = width of fabric

PINK

- Cut 7 sets of 2 squares 4⅞″ × 4⅞″ (14 total).
- Cut 7 sets of 4 squares 2½″ × 2½″ (28 total).

GREEN

- Cut 6 sets of 2 squares 4⅞″ × 4⅞″ (12 total).
- Cut 6 sets of 4 squares 2½″ × 2½″ (24 total).

TURQUOISE, YELLOW, AND ORANGE

From each color:

- Cut 4 sets of 2 squares 4⅞″ × 4⅞″.
- Cut 4 sets of 4 squares 2½″ × 2½″.

WHITE PRINT

- Cut 48 squares 2½″ × 2½″.

DARK TURQUOISE

- Cut 4 strips 4⅞″ × WOF.

  Subcut into 26 squares 4⅞″ × 4⅞″.

- Cut 8 strips 2½″ × WOF.

  Subcut 1 strip into 13 squares 2½″ × 2½″.

  The remaining 7 strips 2½″ × WOF will be used for double-fold binding.

- Cut 1 strip 8″ × WOF.

  Subcut into 2 squares 8″ × 8″. Cut each square once diagonally.

MEDIUM TURQUOISE

- Cut 1 strip 4⅞″ × WOF.

  Subcut into 8 squares 4⅞″ × 4⅞″.

- Cut 4 strips 2½″ × WOF.

  Subcut into 56 squares 2½″ × 2½″.

LIGHT TURQUOISE

- Cut 2 strips 4⅞″ × WOF.

  Subcut into 16 squares 4⅞″ × 4⅞″.

- Cut 1 strip 2½″ × WOF.

  Subcut into 8 squares 2½″ × 2½″.

- Cut 1 strip 15½″ × WOF.

  Subcut into 1 square 15½″ × 15½″. Cut twice diagonally.

WHITE

- Cut 1 strip 15⅜″ × WOF.

  Subcut into 2 squares 15⅜″ × 15⅜″. Cut each twice diagonally.

INSTRUCTIONS

All seam allowances are ¼".

BLOCK ASSEMBLY

To construct the blocks, refer to Churn Dash Block (page 77).

Follow the block layout diagrams and chart below to group your fabrics into sets before constructing the Churn Dash blocks. Use a variety of colors for the different blocks, but select matching colors for each block.

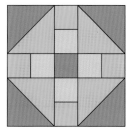
Block A layout

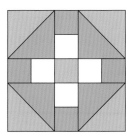
Block B layout

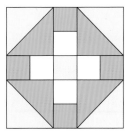
Block C layout

	4⅞" × 4⅞" squares	2½" × 2½" squares	Number to make
BLOCK A	2 colored 2 dark turquoise	4 colored 4 medium turquoise 1 dark turquoise	13
BLOCK B	2 colored 2 medium turquoise	4 colored 4 white print 1 medium turquoise	4
BLOCK C	2 colored 2 light turquoise	4 colored 4 white print 1 light turquoise	8

QUILT CONSTRUCTION

Refer as needed to the instructions for Kim's Deal *Quilt Construction (page 78).*

Assemble the quilt as shown in the *X Marks the Spot* quilt layout diagram (page 90).

QUILTING AND FINISHING

Follow the instructions for *Kim's Deal* Quilting and Finishing (page 79).

About the Designers

Photo by Kalissa Kramer

Mother and daughter **JO KRAMER** and **KELLIE HANKEN** both live in Iowa and coauthored the book *Country Girl Modern: Quilts from the Junction.* Jo blogs about quilting, as well as farm life, audio books, Midwestern food, and beagles, at Jo's Country Junction (joscountryjunction.com). Kelli creates chalk paintings and is pursuing a career in nursing. The design team's work has appeared in many quilting publications—find them at your local newsstand!

Beaded Curtain

MADE BY ALLEGORY LANHAM

When I was little, I wanted a beaded curtain for my bedroom door. I don't remember where I had seen them or even learned of such a thing, but it was always that one missing piece to my perfect bedroom. These days, a quilt inspired by a beaded curtain seems the perfect compromise.

Beaded Curtain is a beginner-friendly quilt made from rectangles and half-square triangles, with a lot of playful design possibilities. By manipulating the placement of these two basic shapes, fun designs suited for kids and Christmas emerge (*Candy Blocks* and *Paper Crackers*), while the striped variation is great for using up both fat quarters and jelly roll strips. Whether made from a single collection or a pile of scraps, any of these quilts could come together easily in a weekend.

FINISHED BLOCK SIZE: 6″ × 14″   •   FINISHED QUILT SIZE: 48½″ × 70½″

MATERIALS

- **Prints:** 20 assorted fat quarters (A mix of 4 or 5 colors works well.)
- **Background:** 1½ yards
- **Binding:** ⅝ yard
- **Backing:** 3⅛ yards
- **Batting:** 56″ × 78″
- **Water-soluble marking pen**

CUTTING

WOF = width of fabric

PRINTS

From each fat quarter:

- Cut 1 strip 6½″ × 20″.

  Subcut into 2 rectangles 6½″ × 8½″ for bead centers.

- Cut 1 strip 4½″ × 20″.

  Subcut into 4 squares 4½″ × 4½″ for half-square triangles.

BACKGROUND

- Cut 10 strips 4½″ × WOF.

  Subcut into 80 squares 4½″ × 4½″ for half-square triangles.

BINDING

- Cut 7 strips 2½″ × WOF for double-fold binding.

INSTRUCTIONS

All seams are ¼" and pressed open.

FLYING GEESE UNITS

1. Using a ruler and a water-soluble marking pen, draw a line down the diagonal center on the wrong side of each 4½" × 4½" background square.

2. Pair a 4½" × 4½" background square and a 4½" × 4½" print square to make 160 half-square triangle units (see Half-Square Triangles, page 55).

> *tip* I highly recommend chain piecing your squares. Draw diagonal lines on all the background squares and pair them all with the print squares. Run all the squares through your machine, one after the other without stopping, sewing on one side of the line. Then flip and run them all back through again, sewing on the other side of the line.

3. Square-up each unit so it measures 3½" × 3½". Make a total of 160 half-square triangles.

4. Group the half-square triangles into matching pairs. Sew together each set along the print edges of the squares to make Flying Geese. These units will become the tops and bottoms of your bead blocks. Make 80 units (4 from each print).

BLOCK ASSEMBLY

1. To create each bead block, you'll need 2 matching Flying Geese units and a 6½" × 8½" rectangle in a different print. Sew a Flying Geese unit to each rectangle along its short side. Check that when the block is pressed open, the point is facing away from the center section.

Bead block layout

2. Keep sewing Flying Geese to center rectangles until you have 40 bead blocks. The bead blocks will measure 6½" × 14½" unfinished.

QUILT CONSTRUCTION

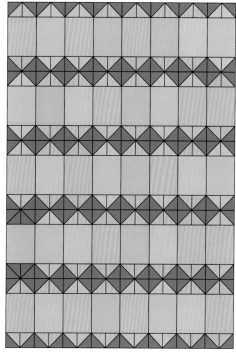

Beaded Curtain quilt layout

1. Arrange the blocks in 8 columns of 5 blocks as shown in the *Beaded Curtain* quilt layout diagram. Distribute the print fabrics evenly.

2. Sew together blocks into vertical columns first to help keep the points lined up.

3. Sew together the columns to finish the quilt top.

QUILTING AND FINISHING

1. Mark quilting designs on the quilt top or plan to stitch without marking.

2. Layer the backing, batting, and quilt top. Use your preferred method to baste together the 3 layers.

3. Quilt as desired.

4. Bind the quilt.

Staggered Columns

FINISHED BLOCK SIZE: 6" × 14" and 6" × 7" • FINISHED QUILT SIZE: 48½" × 70½"

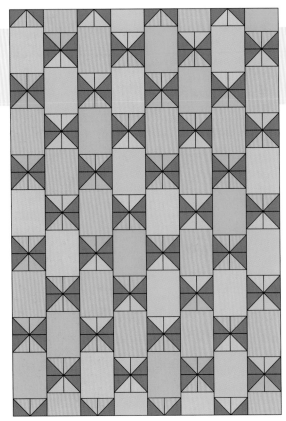

Staggered Columns **quilt layout**

MATERIALS

Follow the materials list from *Beaded Curtain* (page 92).

CUTTING

WOF = width of fabric

Follow the instructions for *Beaded Curtain* (page 93), except:

PRINTS

From each fat quarter:

- Cut 1 strip 6½" × 20".

  Subcut 36 rectangles 6½" × 8½" for full-sized bead centers.

From 8 fat quarters, cut 8 rectangles 6½" × 4½" for half-sized bead centers.

  NOTE: Be sure to evenly distribute the fabrics when cutting the rectangles.

INSTRUCTIONS

All seams are ¼" and pressed open.

BLOCK ASSEMBLY

1. Follow the instructions for Flying Geese Units (page 93). Make 80.

2. Follow the instructions for *Beaded Curtain* Block Assembly (page 93). Make 36 full-sized bead blocks.

3. For the half-sized blocks, attach 1 Flying Geese unit to each 6½" × 4½" rectangle. Half-sized bead blocks will measure 6½" × 7½" unfinished. Make 8.

QUILT CONSTRUCTION

1. Arrange the blocks as shown in the *Staggered Columns* quilt layout diagram. This layout is constructed in 8 columns. Odd-numbered columns have 5 full blocks in them, just as in *Beaded Curtain*.

2. Make the even-numbered columns by sewing together 4 full-sized bead blocks. Add a half-sized block to the top and bottom of the 4 full-sized blocks, matching the points of the Flying Geese units.

3. Sew all columns together to complete the quilt top.

4. Follow the instructions for *Beaded Curtain* Quilting and Finishing (page 93).

Alternating Rows

FINISHED BLOCK SIZE: 6″ × 14″   •   FINISHED QUILT SIZE: 48½″ × 66½″

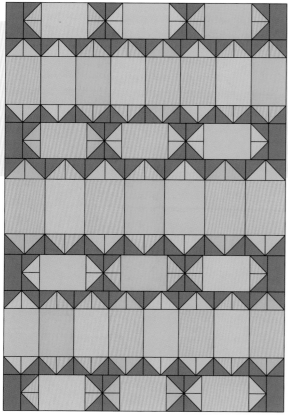

Alternating Rows quilt layout

MATERIALS

Follow the materials list for *Beaded Curtain* (page 92).

Replace the prints with:

- 18 assorted fat quarters of various prints

Increase the background fabric to 1⅝ yards.

CUTTING

WOF = width of fabric

Follow the cutting instructions for *Beaded Curtain* (page 92).

ADD:

- From the background fabric, cut 1 strip 6½″ × WOF.

  Subcut into 8 rectangles 3½″ × 6½″ for horizontal row sashing.

INSTRUCTIONS

All seams are ¼″ and pressed open.

BLOCK ASSEMBLY

1. Follow the instructions for Flying Geese Units (page 93). Make 72.

2. Follow the instructions for *Beaded Curtain* Block Assembly (page 93). Make 36 blocks.

QUILT CONSTRUCTION

1. Arrange the blocks as shown in the *Alternating Rows* quilt layout diagram (above). The orientation of the bead blocks in this quilt alternates between vertical and horizontal.

2. Sew together 8 blocks with the beads arranged vertically. Make 3 rows.

3. Sew together 3 blocks with the beads arranged horizontally and with a sashing rectangle 3½″ × 6½″ added to the ends of each row. Make 4 rows.

4. Sew together the rows as shown in the *Alternating Rows* quilt layout diagram.

5. Follow the instructions for *Beaded Curtain* Quilting and Finishing (page 93).

Columns on Point

FINISHED BLOCK SIZE: 6″ × 12″ • FINISHED QUILT SIZE: 51½″ × 68½″

Columns on Point quilt layout

MATERIALS

- **Prints:** 18 assorted fat quarters
- **Background:** 2¾ yards
- **Binding:** ⅔ yard
- **Backing:** 3¼ yards
- **Batting:** 59″ × 76″

CUTTING

WOF = width of fabric

PRINTS

From each fat quarter:

- Cut 1 strip 6½″ × 20″.

  Subcut into 2 squares 6½″ × 6½″ for bead centers.

- Cut 1 strip 4½″ × 20″.

  Subcut into 4 squares 4½″ × 4½″ for half-square triangles.

BACKGROUND

- Cut 10 strips 4½″ × WOF.

  Subcut into 72 squares 4½″ × 4½″ for half-square triangles.

- Cut 1 strip 9⅜″ × WOF.

  Subcut into 2 squares 9⅜″ × 9⅜″ for corner setting triangles. Then cut on the diagonal to make 4 corner setting triangles.

- Cut 2 strips 18¼″ × WOF.

  Subcut into 4 squares 18¼″ × 18¼″ for side setting triangles. Then cut on the diagonal twice to make 12 side setting triangles. (You will use 10 for this layout.)

BINDING

- Cut 7 strips 2½″ × WOF for double-fold binding.

INSTRUCTIONS

All seams are ¼″ and pressed open.

BLOCK ASSEMBLY

1. Follow the directions for Flying Geese Units (page 93). Make 72.

2. Follow the instructions for *Beaded Curtain* Block Assembly (page 93). Because your center sections are shorter, these bead blocks will measure 6½″ × 12½″ unfinished. Make 36.

3. After making bead blocks, match them up in groups of 2. Sew together 2 bead blocks to create a square unit 12½″ × 12½″. Make 18.

QUILT CONSTRUCTION

1. Arrange the blocks as shown in the *Columns on Point* layout diagram (above). You need 2 diagonal rows of 5 squares, 2 diagonal rows of 3 squares, and 2 diagonal rows with 1 square in each.

2. To the 5-square rows, add a corner setting triangle to the top of a row. To the second 5-square row, add a corner setting triangle to the bottom of this row. Make sure you are sewing the longest side of your corner triangle to your squares.

3. Add side setting triangles to the ends of the 5-square rows without the corner triangles. These side setting triangles are sewn to the squares on one of their short sides.

4. Add side setting triangles to the top and bottom of each 3-square row and to the single squares.

5. To the side of each single-square row, add a single corner setting triangle.

6. Sew together the rows, matching the seams of the bead squares.

7. Follow the instructions for *Beaded Curtain* Quilting and Finishing (page 93).

Striped Centers

FINISHED BLOCK SIZE: 6″ × 14″   •   FINISHED QUILT SIZE: 48½″ × 70½″

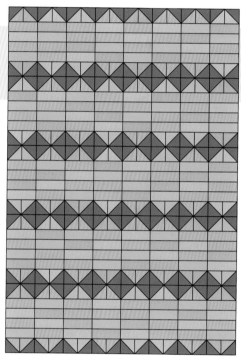

Striped Centers quilt layout

INSTRUCTIONS

All seams are ¼″ and pressed open.

BLOCK ASSEMBLY

Refer as needed to the instructions for Beaded Curtain *Block Assembly (page 93).*

1. Follow the instructions for Flying Geese Units (page 93). Make 80.

2. Mix and match the 2½″ × 6½″ rectangles into groups of 4. Sew together each group of 4 to create a 6½″ × 8½″ rectangle. These 6½″ × 8½″ rectangles will now be your bead center unit. Make 40.

MATERIALS

Follow the materials list for *Beaded Curtain* (page 92).

CUTTING

Follow the cutting instructions for *Beaded Curtain* (page 92), except:

PRINTS

From each fat quarter:

- Cut 1 strip 4½″ × 20″.

  Subcut into 4 squares 4½″ × 4½″ for half-square triangles.

- Cut 1 strip 6½″ × 20″.

  Subcut into 8 strips 2½″ × 6½″ for pieced bead centers.

3. Join a Flying Geese unit to each short end of the 6½″ × 8½″ rectangles. Make 40.

Striped Centers block layout

QUILT CONSTRUCTION

1. Arrange the blocks as shown in the *Striped Centers* quilt layout diagram (above).

2. Follow the instructions for *Beaded Curtain* Quilt Construction (page 93).

3. Follow the instructions for *Beaded Curtain* Quilting and Finishing (page 93).

Candy Blocks

FINISHED BLOCK SIZE: 6″ × 14″ • FINISHED QUILT SIZE: 48½″ × 70½″

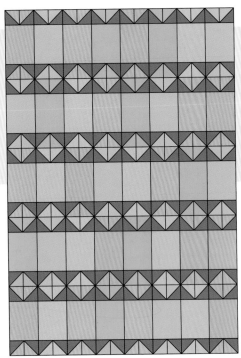

Candy Blocks quilt layout

MATERIALS

Follow the materials list for *Beaded Curtain* (page 92).

CUTTING

Follow the cutting instructions for *Beaded Curtain* (page 92).

INSTRUCTIONS

All seams are ¼″ and pressed open.

BLOCK ASSEMBLY

Refer as needed to the instructions for Beaded Curtain *Block Assembly (page 93).*

1. Follow the instructions for Flying Geese Units (page 93). Make 80.

2. To create each candy block, you will need 2 matching Flying Geese units and a matching rectangle print 6½″ × 8½″. Sew a Flying Geese unit to each 6½″-long side of the center rectangle. Make sure that when the block is pressed open, the point is facing toward the center section. Make 40.

QUILT CONSTRUCTION

1. Arrange the blocks as shown in the *Candy Blocks* quilt layout diagram (at left).

2. Follow the instructions for *Beaded Curtain* Quilt Construction (page 93).

3. Follow the instructions for *Beaded Curtain* Quilting and Finishing (page 93).

Paper Crackers

FINISHED BLOCK SIZE: 6″ × 20″ • FINISHED QUILT SIZE: 66½″ × 84½″

Paper Crackers quilt layout

The extra half-square triangles turn this block into a festive holiday design inspired by Christmas paper crackers.

MATERIALS

- **Prints:** 21 assorted fat quarters (A mix of red and green is recommended.)

- **Background:** 3½ yards
- **Binding:** ¾ yard
- **Backing:** 5 yards
- **Batting:** 74″ × 92″

CUTTING

WOF = width of fabric

PRINTS

From each fat quarter:

- Cut 2 strips 4½″ × 20″.

    Subcut into 8 squares 4½″ × 4½″ for half-square triangles.

- Cut 1 strip 6½″ × 20″.

    Subcut into 2 rectangles 6½″ × 8½″ for centers.

BACKGROUND

- Cut 21 strips 4½″ × WOF.

    Subcut into 168 squares 4½″ × 4½″ for half-square triangles.

- Cut 3 strips 6½″ × WOF.

    Subcut into 42 rectangles 2½″ × 6½″ for block sashing.

BINDING

- Cut 9 strips 2½″ × WOF for double-fold binding.

INSTRUCTIONS

BLOCK ASSEMBLY

1. Follow the instructions for Flying Geese Units (page 93). Make 168.

2. Make block ends by sewing together 2 Flying Geese units of the same print fabric, with points matching and facing each other. Repeat until you have 84 block ends.

3. Match 2 block ends with 1 block center rectangle 6½″ × 8½″. Sew a block end to either side of a center rectangle.

 Paper Crackers block layout

4. Repeat Step 3 with the other rectangle centers to create 42 blocks.

QUILT CONSTRUCTION

1. Arrange the blocks as shown in the *Paper Crackers* quilt layout diagram (page 99), alternating red and green blocks. This quilt has 14 rows.

2. To create the staggered effect, add background fabric sashing pieces 2½″ × 6½″. The pattern for odd-numbered rows is sashing, block, sashing, block, sashing, block. The pattern for even-numbered rows is block, sashing, block, sashing, block, sashing.

3. Sew together the rows to finish the quilt top.

4. Follow the instructions for *Beaded Curtain* Quilting and Finishing (page 93).

Arrow Blocks

FINISHED BLOCK SIZE: **14″ × 6″** • FINISHED QUILT SIZE: **56½″ × 72½″**

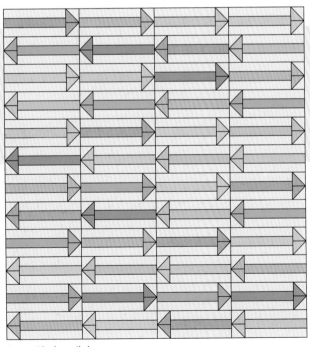

Arrow Blocks **quilt layout**

MATERIALS

- **Prints:** 12 assorted fat quarters
- **Background:** 3½ yards
- **Binding:** ⅝ yard
- **Backing:** 3½ yards
- **Batting:** 64″ × 80″

CUTTING

WOF = width of fabric

PRINTS

From each fat quarter:

- Cut 1 strip 4½″ × 20″.

  Subcut into 4 squares 4½″ × 4½″ for half-square triangles.

- Cut 4 rectangles 2½″ × 11½″ for arrow ends.

BACKGROUND

- Cut 6 strips 4½" × WOF.

    Subcut into 48 squares 4½" × 4½" for half-square triangles.

- Cut 33 strips 2½" × WOF.

    Subcut into 98 rectangles 2½" × 11½" for arrow ends.

BINDING

- Cut 7 strips 1½" × WOF for double-fold binding.

INSTRUCTIONS

All seams are ¼" and pressed open.

BLOCK ASSEMBLY

Refer as needed to the instructions for Beaded Curtain *block assembly (page 93).*

1. Follow the instructions for Flying Geese Units (page 93). These Flying Geese units will be the arrow tops. Make 48.

2. Make arrow ends from 1 print strip 2½" × 11½" and 2 background rectangles 2½" × 11½". Sew a background strip on either side of the print strip to create a 6½" × 11½" rectangle. Make 48.

3. Sew each arrow top to its matching arrow end to make 48 blocks.

Arrow Blocks
block layout

QUILT CONSTRUCTION

1. This variation consists of 12 rows, each containing 4 blocks. Mix up the different prints to get an even distribution throughout the quilt. Sew together each row of 4 blocks.

2. As you join the rows, flip the blocks so that the arrows alternate pointing to the right and pointing to the left, as shown in the *Arrow Blocks* quilt layout diagram (page 100).

3. Sew together the rows to finish the quilt top.

4. Follow the instructions for *Beaded Curtain* Quilting and Finishing (page 93).

About the Designer

Photo by Allegory Lanham

ALLEGORY LANHAM grew up outside of Paducah, Kentucky, where she started garment sewing in her teens and quickly found quilting. She lives near Atlanta, Georgia, now and travels throughout the South teaching classes on everything from English paper piecing to quilt-as-you-go techniques. Allegory shares patterns and projects on her website, A Thousand Needles (athousandneedles.com).

Au Contraire

MADE BY ELLEN MURPHY

This simple wallhanging looks complex, but it is made from just one quilt block, Contrary Wife. Some of the blocks are rotated and some use different color combinations, but all the designs are built from one simple block.

FINISHED BLOCK SIZE: 9" × 9"   •   FINISHED QUILT SIZE: 39½" × 39½"

MATERIALS AND CUTTING

WOF = width of fabric

FABRIC REQUIREMENTS	AMOUNT NEEDED	CUTTING
FABRIC A: DARK RED	2 fat quarters	4 squares 9″ × 9″ 4 squares 3½″ × 3½″
FABRIC B: LIGHT RED	1 fat quarter	16 squares 3½″ × 3½″
FABRIC C: DARK YELLOW	1 fat quarter	12 squares 3½″ × 3½″
FABRIC D: LIGHT YELLOW	1 fat quarter	8 squares 3½″ × 3½″
FABRIC E: DARK BLUE	1 fat quarter	4 squares 9″ × 9″
FABRIC F: LIGHT BLUE	1 fat quarter ½ yard for border	16 squares 3½″ × 3½″ 5 strips 2″ × WOF
FABRIC G: DARK GREEN	1 fat quarter	12 squares 3½″ × 3½″
FABRIC H: LIGHT GREEN	1 fat quarter	12 squares 3½″ × 3½″
FABRIC I: BACKGROUND	2 fat quarters	8 squares 9″ × 9″
BINDING	⅓ yard	5 strips 2½″ × WOF
BACKING	2⅔ yards of 40″-wide fabric	Piece fabric to 48″ × 48″.
BATTING	48″ × 48″	

INSTRUCTIONS

All seam allowances are ¼″. Follow the instructions for One Simple Block (page 104).

BLOCK ASSEMBLY

For Au Contraire, you will make the Contrary Wife block in four different colorways.

1. Pair white 9″ × 9″ squares with dark red 9″ × 9″ squares to make a total of 16 half-square triangles.

2. Pair white 9″ × 9″ squares with blue 9″ × 9″ squares to make a total of 16 half-square triangles.

3. Arrange solid squares and half-square triangles as shown in the block layout diagrams.

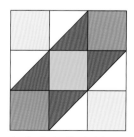

Au Contraire Block A layout: Make 4.

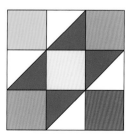

Au Contraire Block B layout: Make 4.

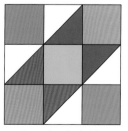

Au Contraire Block C layout: Make 4.

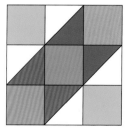

Au Contraire Block D layout: Make 4.

One Simple Block

All the projects in this chapter incorporate one simple block, called Contrary Wife. Refer to these instructions to make this one simple block and a border for all the quilts.

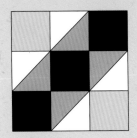

Contrary Wife block

HALF-SQUARE TRIANGLES (8-IN-1 METHOD)

The projects in this chapter rely on the 8-in-1 method for making 8 half-square triangles from a single square.

1. On the back of a 9″ × 9″ background square, mark a diagonal line in each direction. For *Au Contraire*, pair 4 squares of Fabric E with 4 squares of Fabric I. Also pair 4 squares of Fabric A with 4 squares of Fabric I.

2. Sew ¼″ away from each side of the drawn lines.

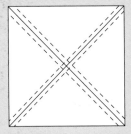

Mark diagonal lines and sew on either side.

3. Cut a vertical line through the center of the square. Cut each rectangle in half with a horizontal cut through the center. Take care when cutting so that the fabric does not shift.

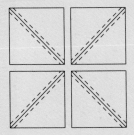

Make vertical and horizontal cuts through square's midpoint.

4. Cut on the drawn diagonal lines in each smaller square unit. Press the seams toward the darker fabric. Square-up your blocks to measure 3½″ × 3½″. (You will trim a small amount from each side.)

BLOCK ASSEMBLY

1. Arrange the colored blocks and half-square triangles as shown. Sew together each row. Press the seams in Rows 1 and 3 to the outside and the seams in Row 2 to the inside.

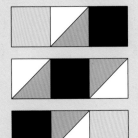

Sew blocks together to form rows.

2. Sew together the rows and press the seams to the outside. Square-up the block to measure 9½″ × 9½″.

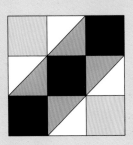

Sew together rows.

QUILT CONSTRUCTION

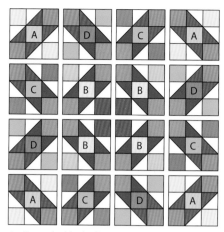

Au Contraire block placement

> **tip** Before sewing together your blocks, stand back and check your placement! The blue stars should form a diagonal shape in the center, the red half stars are around the edge, the green squares should make a diamond shape, and the yellow squares should make diagonal lines. There should also be a red square in the center.

1. Arrange the quilt blocks according to the *Au Contraire* block placement diagram. Once your blocks are placed correctly, sew them together in 4 rows. Press the seams in Rows 1 and 3 to the left and the seams in Rows 2 and 4 to the right.

2. Sew together the rows and press open those seams to reduce bulk.

BORDERS

1. Sew together the 5 strips of light blue border fabric 2″ × WOF along short ends.

2. Measure from top to bottom through the quilt center. Cut 2 strips to this measurement. Sew a border to each side of the quilt. Press the seams toward the border.

3. Measure from side to side through the quilt center, including borders. Cut 2 strips to this measurement. Sew a border to the top and bottom of the quilt. Press seams toward the border.

Au Contraire quilt layout

QUILTING AND FINISHING

1. Mark quilting designs on the quilt top or plan to stitch without marking.

2. Layer the backing, batting, and quilt top. Use your preferred method to baste together the 3 layers.

3. Quilt as desired.

4. Bind the quilt.

Chain Link

FINISHED BLOCK SIZE: 9″ × 9″   •   FINISHED QUILT SIZE: 40½″ × 49½″

Chain Link quilt layout

MATERIALS AND CUTTING

WOF = width of fabric

FABRIC	AMOUNT NEEDED	CUTTING
WHITE	1⅛ yards	10 squares 9″ × 9″
BLACK-AND-WHITE PRINT	1⅜ yards	40 squares 3½″ × 3½″ 10 squares 9″ × 9″
RED	2 fat quarters	40 squares 3½″ × 3½″
LIGHT GRAY	1 fat quarter	10 squares 3½″ × 3½″
MEDIUM GRAY	1 fat quarter	10 squares 3½″ × 3½″
BORDER: BLACK	½ yard	5 strips 2½″ × WOF
BINDING	½ yard	5 strips 2½″ × WOF
BACKING	2⅔ yards	Piece fabric to make backing 46″ × 55″
BATTING	48″ × 57″	

INSTRUCTIONS

All seam allowances are ¼″. Follow the instructions for One Simple Block (page 104). Refer to the Chain Link *quilt layout diagram for block placement. Follow the instructions for* Au Contraire *Quilting and Finishing (page 105).*

BLOCK ASSEMBLY

1. Pair white 9″ × 9″ squares with black-and-white print 9″ × 9″ squares to make 80 half-square triangles.

2. Arrange solid squares and half-square triangles as shown in the block diagrams.

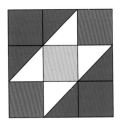

Chain Link Block A layout: Make 10.

Chain Link Block B layout: Make 10.

Big Red

FINISHED BLOCK SIZE: 9″ × 9″ • FINISHED QUILT SIZE: 43½″ × 52½″

Big Red quilt layout

MATERIALS AND CUTTING

WOF = width of fabric

FABRIC	AMOUNT NEEDED	CUTTING
GOLD	2 fat quarters	20 squares 3½″ × 3½″ 4 rectangles 2″ × 10″ 5 rectangles 2″ × 10½″
BLUE	2 fat quarters	20 squares 3½″ × 3½″ 4 rectangles 2″ × 10″ 5 rectangles 2″ × 10½″
RED	1⅜ yards	40 squares 3½″ × 3½″ 10 squares 9″ × 9″
WHITE	1¼ yard	20 squares 3½″ × 3½″ 10 squares 9″ × 9″
GREEN	½ yard	9 strips 1½″ × WOF
BINDING	½ yard	6 strips 2½″ × WOF
BACKING	3 yards	Piece fabric to 51″ × 60″.
BATTING	51″ × 60″	

INSTRUCTIONS

All seam allowances are ¼". Follow the instructions for One Simple Block (page 104). Refer to the Big Red quilt layout diagram for block placement. Follow the instructions for Au Contraire Quilting and Finishing (page 105).

BLOCK ASSEMBLY

1. Pair red 9" × 9" squares with white 9" × 9" squares to make 80 half-square triangles.

2. Arrange solid squares and half-square triangles as shown in the block diagrams.

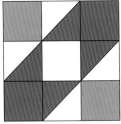

Big Red Block A layout: Make 10.

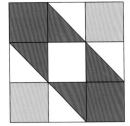

Big Red Block B layout: Make 10.

BORDERS

1. Make the inner and outer borders as instructed in the instructions for *Au Contraire* Borders (page 105).

2. To make the middle border for the top and bottom of the quilt, sew together 2 blue rectangles 2" × 10" with 2 gold rectangles 2" × 10", alternating the colors as shown. Make 2.

Middle border for top and bottom

3. To make the middle border for the left side of the quilt, sew together 3 gold rectangles 2" × 10½" with 2 blue rectangles 2" × 10½", alternating colors as shown. Make 1.

Middle border for left side

4. To make the middle border for the right side of the quilt, sew together 3 blue rectangles 2" × 10½" with 2 gold rectangles 2" × 10½", alternating colors as shown. Make 1.

Middle border for right side

5. Sew each of the borders to the quilt, always sewing the sides first, then the top and bottom.

Magnificent Valor

FINISHED BLOCK SIZE: 9″ × 9″ • FINISHED QUILT SIZE: 54½″ × 63½″

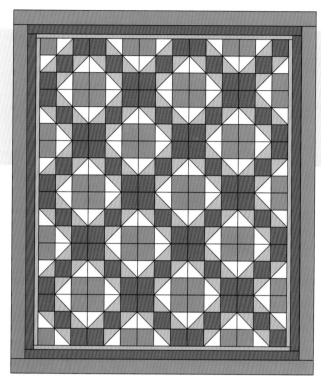

Magnificent Valor quilt layout

tip Use a variety of fat quarters in this quilt for a scrappy look. Mix up your reds and blues to give your quilt more interest and make it sparkle.

MATERIALS AND CUTTING

WOF = width of fabric

FABRIC	AMOUNT NEEDED	CUTTING
BLUE	3 different fat quarters ⅝ yard for the outer border	60 squares 3½″ × 3½″ (20 from each fat quarter) 6 strips 2½″ × WOF
RED	4 different fat quarters ½ yard for the middle border	90 squares 3½″ × 3½″ (23 from 3 of the fat quarters and 21 from the last fat quarter) 6 strips 2″ × WOF
WHITE	1⅛ yards	15 squares 9″ × 9″
GOLD	1½ yards	15 squares 9″ × 9″ 6 strips 1½″ × WOF (for inner border)
BINDING	⅝ yard	7 strips 2½″ × WOF
BACKING	3½ yards	Piece fabric to 62″ × 71″.
BATTING	62″ × 71″	

INSTRUCTIONS

All seam allowances are 1/4". Follow the instructions for One Simple Block (page 104). Refer to the Magnificent Valor quilt layout diagram for block placement. Follow the instructions for Au Contraire Border (page 105) to make the 3 borders. Follow the instructions for Au Contraire Quilting and Finishing (page 105).

BLOCK ASSEMBLY

Pair white 9" × 9" squares with gold 9" × 9" squares to make a total of 120 half-square triangles. Arrange solid squares and half-square triangles as shown in the block layout diagram. Make 30 blocks.

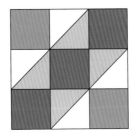

Magnificent Valor block layout

QUILT CONSTRUCTION

Arrange the blocks as shown, rotating every other block by 90°.

Ups and Downs

FINISHED BLOCK SIZE: 9" × 9" • FINISHED QUILT SIZE: 54½" × 63½"

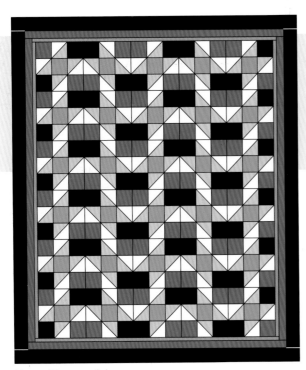

Ups and Downs quilt layout

MATERIALS AND CUTTING

WOF = width of fabric

FABRIC	AMOUNT NEEDED	CUTTING
BLACK	3 fat quarters ⅝ yard (for outer border)	60 squares 3½" × 3½" 2 strips 3½" × WOF
RED	3 fat quarters ½ yard (for middle border)	60 squares 3½" × 3½" 6 strips 2" × WOF
MEDIUM GRAY	2 fat quarters	30 squares 3½" × 3½"
WHITE	1⅛ yards	15 squares 9" × 9"
LIGHT GRAY	1⅛ yards	15 squares 9" × 9" 6 strips 1½" × WOF (for inner border)
BINDING	⅝ yard	7 strips 2½" × WOF
BACKING	3½ yards	Piece fabric to 62" × 71".
BATTING	62" × 71"	

INSTRUCTIONS

All seam allowances are ¼". Follow the instructions for One Simple Block (page 104). Refer to the Ups and Downs quilt layout diagram for block placement. Follow the instructions for Au Contraire Border (page 105) to make the 3 borders. Follow the instructions for Au Contraire Quilting and Finishing (page 105).

BLOCK ASSEMBLY

Pair white 9" × 9" squares with light gray 9" × 9" squares to make a total of 120 half-square triangles. Arrange solid squares and half-square triangles as shown in the block layout diagram. Make 30.

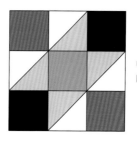

Ups and Downs block layout

QUILT CONSTRUCTION

Arrange the blocks as shown. Focus on the diagonal lines made by the gray fabrics to help place the blocks properly.

Garden Paths

FINISHED BLOCK SIZE: 9" × 9"   •   FINISHED QUILT SIZE: 49" × 59½"

Garden Paths quilt layout

MATERIALS AND CUTTING

WOF = width of fabric

FABRIC	AMOUNT NEEDED	CUTTING
PINK	2 fat quarters	40 squares 3½" × 3½"
BLUE	2 fat quarters	40 squares 3½" × 3½"
PURPLE	1 fat quarter	20 squares 3½" × 3½"
GREEN	1⅛ yards	30 squares 2" × 2" 10 squares 9" × 9"
WHITE	1⅜ yards	10 squares 9" × 9" 49 rectangles 2" × 3½"
LIGHT YELLOW	¾ yard	98 rectangles 2" × 3½"
BORDER	⅝ yard	6 strips 3" × WOF
BINDING	½ yard	6 strips 2½" × WOF
BACKING	3¼ yards	Piece fabric to 57" × 67".
BATTING	57" × 67"	

INSTRUCTIONS

All seam allowances are ¼". Follow the instructions for One Simple Block (page 104). Refer to the Garden Paths quilt layout diagram for block placement. Follow the instructions for Au Contraire Border (page 105) to make the border. Follow the instructions for Au Contraire Quilting and Finishing (page 105).

BLOCK ASSEMBLY

Pair green 9" × 9" squares with white 9" × 9" squares to make a total of 80 half-square triangles. Arrange solid squares and half-square triangles as shown in the block layout diagram. Make 20.

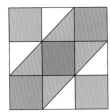

Garden Paths block layout

SASHING AND CORNERSTONES

1. Sew together 2 yellow 2" × 3½" rectangles with 1 white 2" × 3½" rectangle as shown to make a sashing unit. Press seams to the outside. Make 49.

Sashing units

2. Sew 5 green 2" × 2" squares to 4 sashing units as shown. Make 6.

Sashing strip

QUILT CONSTRUCTION

Arrange the blocks as shown, rotating every other block by 90°.

About the Designer

Photo by Avalon

ELLEN MURPHY says she was born with a crayon in her hand and has always loved art, craft, and color. She lives in Indiana and is the author of *American Homestead Quilts* and *American Homestead Christmas* (both from C&T Publishing). Ellen has a degree in fine art and works both as a graphic designer and as a quilting instructor. Many of her designs reflect the folk art of her European roots. She blogs about quilting and travel and is the owner of American Homestead (americanhomesteaddesign.com), a craft pattern design company.

Sunshine on a Cloudy Day

PIECED BY ALLISON NICOLL
QUILTED BY JAN WAND

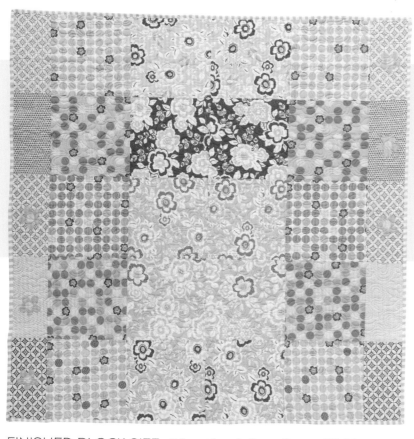

If you have a fat quarter bundle that you love so much you can't bear to cut it up, then this is the project for you. Big, bold prints are perfect for this fun and fast quilt. The appliqué adds a little pop. Grab your fat quarter bundle and let's get stitching!

FINISHED BLOCK SIZE: 12″ × 12″ and 6″ × 12″ • FINISHED QUILT SIZE: 60½″ × 60½″

MATERIALS

- **Prints:** 10 matching pairs of fat quarters and 5 single fat quarters

- **Felt scraps for appliqué flowers**

- **Paper-backed fusible webbing:** ½ yard

- **Batting:** 65″ × 65″

- **Backing:** 3¾ yards

- **Binding:** ⅝ yard

CUTTING

WOF = width of fabric

PRINTS

- Cut 1 square 12½″ × 12½″ from each of the 20 matching fat quarters.

- Cut 2 rectangles 6½″ × 12½″ from each of 5 single fat quarters.

BINDING

- Cut 7 strips 2½″ × WOF for double-fold binding.

INSTRUCTIONS

QUILT CONSTRUCTION

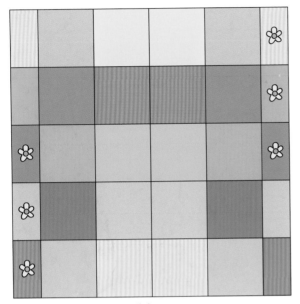

Sunshine on a Cloudy Day **quilt layout**

1. Place the squares into 5 rows of 4 squares, as shown in the quilt layout diagram. Place the 6½" × 12½" rectangles at the beginning and end of each row. Move the pieces around until you are happy with the design.

> *tip* It's helpful to have a large surface when you are deciding how to arrange your blocks. Try out different layouts until you are pleased with the result.

2. Sew together the blocks to form rows. Sew together the rows.

3. Trace 6 flowers and 6 centers using the patterns (page 119) onto the paper side of the fusible webbing. Use paper scissors to cut out the drawn shapes, adding an ⅛" border around each shape.

4. Fuse the cut shapes to the wrong side of the felt scraps using a hot, dry iron according to the manufacturer's instructions.

> *tip* Press firmly with your iron when fusing the shapes to the felt.

5. Cut around the shapes on your original, traced line. Then remove the paper backing and fuse the shapes to your quilt as shown in the *Sunshine on a Cloudy Day* quilt layout diagram.

6. Use the blanket stitch setting on your sewing machine to sew around the appliqué shapes. Use a coordinating thread so that the stitches blend in.

QUILTING AND FINISHING

1. Cut the backing fabric in half crosswise. Sew together the pieces lengthwise.

2. Layer the backing, batting, and quilt top. Use your preferred method to baste the 3 layers together.

3. Quilt using an allover swirl design. My quilt was quilted on a longarm sewing machine.

4. Bind the quilt.

Raw-Edge Appliqué

Instead of fusing felt scraps, you can change the look by using fabric scraps and raw-edge appliqué.

- To do raw-edge appliqué, you need a free-motion foot (also called a darning foot) for your machine. Sewing machine dealers offer various kinds. I prefer an open-toe foot when doing raw-edge appliqué, as it makes it easier to get close to the fabric's edge.

- It's essential to lower the feed dogs on your machine for this free-motion technique. Check your sewing machine manual if you aren't sure how to do this.

- I like to use thread that matches my fabrics so the stitches blend.

- Stitch around each shape three times, sewing as close to the edge as possible so that the edges are stitched down completely. Over time there will be some slight fraying, but the appliqués will stay in place.

Snuggle Up Cuddle Pie

FINISHED BLOCK SIZE: **12″ × 12″ and 12″ × 6″** • FINISHED QUILT SIZE: **48½″ × 60½″**

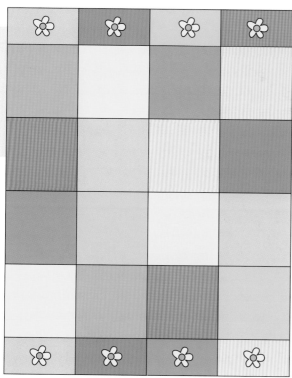

Snuggle Up Cuddle Pie quilt layout

This quilt is slightly smaller when finished, but what really makes it stand out from the rest is that it is backed in soft fleece. The result is a softer, more snuggly quilt with no batting needed. It's become a favorite technique of mine!

MATERIALS

Follow the materials list for *Sunshine on a Cloudy Day* (page 113), except:

Remove the batting.

Replace the prints, batting, backing, and binding with:

- **Prints:** 20 fat quarters
- **Backing:** 1⅔ yards of 60″-wide fleece
- **Binding:** ½ yard

CUTTING

FAT QUARTERS

- Cut 1 square 12½″ × 12½″ from each of 16 fat quarters.
- Cut 2 rectangles 6½″ × 12½″ from each of 4 fat quarters.

BINDING

- Cut 6 strips 2½″ × WOF for double-fold binding.

INSTRUCTIONS

All seam allowances are ¼″.

QUILT CONSTRUCTION

Follow the instructions for *Sunshine on a Cloudy Day* Quilt Construction (page 114).

1. Change the layout by placing the squares into 4 rows of 4 squares each. Add a row of 4 rectangles 6½″ × 12½″ to the top and bottom of the quilt.

2. Increase the number of flowers and flower centers to 8.

3. Arrange the blocks as shown in the *Snuggle Up Cuddle Pie* quilt layout diagram.

QUILTING AND FINISHING

Follow the instructions for *Sunshine on a Cloudy Day* Quilting and Finishing (page 114), but skip the batting layer when basting the quilt.

Sweet Little Petal

FINISHED BLOCK SIZE: 12″ × 12″ and 12″ × 6″   •   FINISHED QUILT SIZE: 36½″ × 48½″

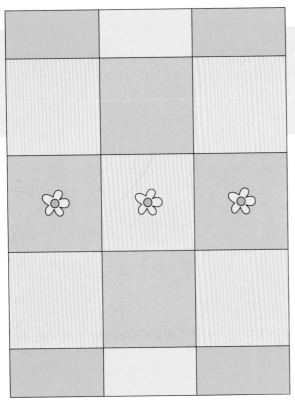

Sweet Little Petal quilt layout

I always seem to need to make a baby quilt for someone. This fast, fun design can be done in a weekend. And who doesn't swoon over a new baby snuggled under a handmade quilt?

MATERIALS

- **Prints:** 12 fat quarters
- **Felt scraps for appliqué flowers**
- **Paper-backed fusible webbing:** ¼ yard
- **Batting:** 41″ × 53″
- **Backing:** 1½ yards
- **Binding:** ½ yard

CUTTING

WOF = width of fabric

PRINTS

- Cut 1 square 12½″ × 12½″ from each of 9 fat quarters.
- Cut 2 rectangles 6½″ × 12½″ from each of 3 fat quarters.

BINDING

- Cut 5 strips 2½″ × WOF for double-fold binding.

INSTRUCTIONS

All seam allowances are ¼″.

QUILT CONSTRUCTION

Follow the instructions for *Sunshine on a Cloudy Day* Quilt Construction (page 114).

1. Change the layout by placing the squares into 3 rows of 3 squares each. Add a row of 3 rectangles 6½″ × 12½″ to the top and bottom of the quilt.

2. Reduce the number of flowers and flower centers to 3.

3. Arrange the blocks as shown in the *Sweet Little Petal* quilt layout diagram.

QUILTING AND FINISHING

Follow the instructions for *Sunshine on a Cloudy Day* Quilting and Finishing (page 114).

Wish Upon a Star

FINISHED BLOCK SIZE: 12″ × 12″ and 12″ × 6″ • FINISHED QUILT SIZE: 36½″ × 48½″

Wish Upon a Star quilt layout

This baby quilt is perfect for a little boy. Use a soft color palette. For the appliqué stars, consider using a fabric that has gold or silver foil for a star that really shimmers.

MATERIALS

Follow the materials list for *Sweet Little Petal* (page 116).

CUTTING

Follow the cutting instructions for *Sweet Little Petal* (page 116).

INSTRUCTIONS

All seam allowances are ¼″.

QUILT CONSTRUCTION

Follow the instructions for *Sunshine on a Cloudy Day* Quilt Construction (page 114).

1. Change the layout by placing the squares into 3 rows of 3 squares each. Add a row of 3 rectangles 6½″ × 12½″ to the top and bottom of the quilt.

2. Replace the flowers with the star appliqués and trace 3 using the pattern (page 119).

3. Arrange the blocks as shown in the *Wish Upon a Star* quilt layout diagram.

QUILTING AND FINISHING

Follow the instructions for *Sunshine on a Cloudy Day* Quilting and Finishing (page 114).

Pom-Pom Party

FINISHED BLOCK SIZE: 12″ × 12″ and 12″ × 6″ • FINISHED QUILT SIZE: 54½″ × 66½″

Pom-Pom Party quilt layout

This quilt is so fun. Changing up the fabrics and adding a pom-pom trim gives it a totally new look. I also added a border to this design.

MATERIALS

- **Prints:** 20 fat quarters
- **Batting:** 60″ × 72″
- **Backing:** 3⅓ yards
- **Binding:** ⅝ yard
- **Border:** ⅞ yard
- **Pom-pom trim:** 7 yards

CUTTING

WOF = width of fabric

PRINTS

- Cut 1 square 12½″ × 12½″ from each of 16 fat quarters.
- Cut 2 rectangles 6½″ × 12½″ from each of 4 fat quarters.

BORDER

- Cut 7 strips 3½″ × WOF.

BINDING

- Cut 7 strips 2½″ × WOF for double-fold binding.

INSTRUCTIONS

All seam allowances are ¼″.

QUILT CONSTRUCTION

Follow the instructions for *Sunshine on a Cloudy Day* Quilt Construction (page 114).

1. Change the layout by placing the squares into 4 rows of 4 squares each. Add a row of 4 rectangles 6½″ × 12½″ to the top and bottom of the quilt.

2. Skip the directions involving appliqué shapes.

3. Arrange the blocks as shown in the *Pom-Pom Party* quilt layout diagram.

4. Sew border strips end to end.

5. Stitch the border to both sides of the quilt top, trimming off the excess as you go. Repeat this step with the top and bottom borders.

QUILTING AND FINISHING

Follow the instructions for *Sunshine on a Cloudy Day* Quilting and Finishing (page 114). Around the outside of the quilt, baste the pom-pom trim in place with the pom-poms facing toward the inside of the quilt. Then, add the binding.

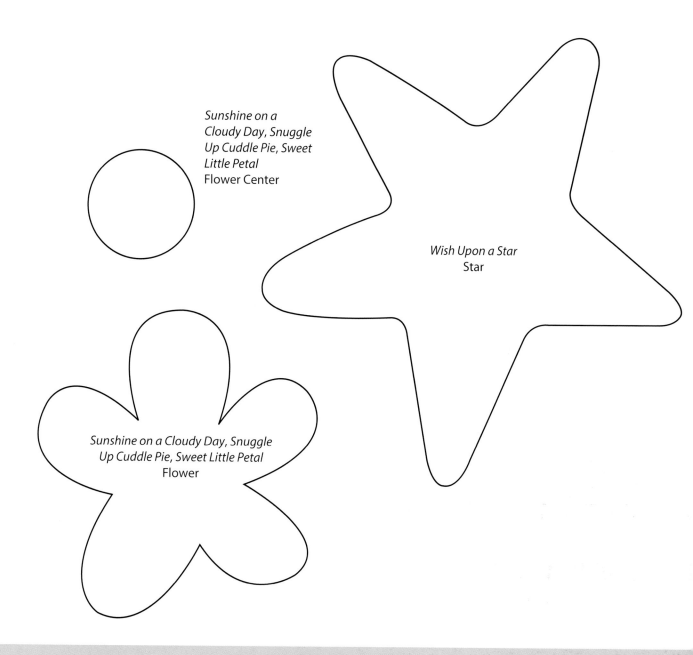

*Sunshine on a
Cloudy Day, Snuggle
Up Cuddle Pie, Sweet
Little Petal*
Flower Center

Wish Upon a Star
Star

*Sunshine on a Cloudy Day, Snuggle
Up Cuddle Pie, Sweet Little Petal*
Flower

About the Designer

ALLISON NICOLL lives in Sydney, Australia, and makes her quilts in her dining area while surrounded by her three sons. She is the author of *Sew It!* (from FunStitch Studio, an imprint of C&T Publishing), a book that teaches kids how to sew. Several of her quilt designs have been featured in international magazines. She loves fun, fresh, simple designs and is drawn to bold prints, including florals, polka dots, and big motifs. "Making a quilt shouldn't be a stressful thing," she says. "It should be relaxing and enjoyable. To make a quilt is to make something filled with love."

Photo by Liz Crocombe, Cutie Patootie Photographie

Steps and Stairs

MADE BY SUE PFAU

I gravitate toward simple designs, and I like to keep fabric selection easy. With this pattern, you can pick up a bundle of fat quarters and make a complete quilt! By adding sashing and borders, you have several choices of sizes to make. I love this pattern because you can rotate the blocks for a myriad of looks.

FINISHED BLOCK SIZE: 9″ × 9″ • FINISHED QUILT SIZE: 64½″ × 86½″

MATERIALS

- **Medium or dark:** 12 fat quarters
- **Cream:** 3 yards (for blocks and sashing)
- **Binding:** ¾ yard
- **Backing:** 5¼ yards
- **Batting:** 71″ × 93″

INSTRUCTIONS

All seam allowances are ¼".

CUTTING

WOF = width of fabric

MEDIUM OR DARK

From each of the 12 fat quarters:

- Cut 4 strips 3½" × 20". From each strip, subcut:

  1 square 3½" × 3½"

  1 rectangle 3½" × 6½"

  1 rectangle 3½" × 9½"

- Sort the squares and rectangles into 48 matching sets of 1 square 3½" × 3½", 1 rectangle 3½" × 6½", and 1 rectangle 3½" × 9½".

From the remaining fat quarter fabric:

- Cut 35 squares 2½" × 2½" for cornerstones.

CREAM

- Cut 13 strips 3½" × WOF.

  Subcut into 48 squares 3½" × 3½" for blocks.

  Subcut into 48 rectangles 3½" × 6½" for blocks.

- Cut 21 strips 2½ " × WOF.

  Subcut into 82 rectangles 2½" × 9½" for sashing.

BINDING

- Cut 9 strips 2½" × WOF for double-fold binding.

BLOCK ASSEMBLY

1. Sew 1 colored square 3½" × 3½" to 1 cream strip 3½" × 6½". Sew the matching colored 3½" × 6½" strip to a cream 3½" × 3½" square. Press toward the darker fabric. Repeat for all 48 matching sets of fabric.

Sew together strips and squares to make 48.

2. Arrange the block as shown in the Steps and Stairs block layout diagram. Add a matching colored strip 3½" × 9½" to the bottom and sew together the units lengthwise. Press the seam allowances in the same direction. Make 48 blocks.

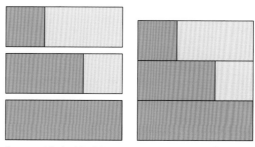

Steps and Stairs block layout

QUILT CONSTRUCTION

1. Arrange the blocks in 8 rows, with 6 blocks in each row. Place a sashing strip 2½" × 9½" between each pair of blocks. There are many ways to arrange the blocks, so try different placements before you settle on a design. The *Steps and Stairs* quilt layout diagram shows how I arranged mine.

2. Sew the blocks and sashing strips into rows. Press the seam allowances toward the block.

3. To make the sashing, sew together sashing strips 2½" × 9½" and colored squares 2½" × 2½", rotating them as shown in the *Steps and Stairs* sashing strip layout diagram (page 122). Each row will have 6 sashing strips and 5 colored squares. Press the seam allowances toward the squares. Make 7.

Steps and Stairs sashing strip layout

4. Place a row of sashing between each two rows of blocks. Sew together the rows to form the quilt top. Press the seam allowances toward the sashing strips.

Steps and Stairs quilt layout

QUILTING AND FINISHING

1. Mark quilting designs on the quilt top or plan to stitch without marking.

2. Layer the backing, batting, and quilt top. Use your preferred method to baste together the 3 layers.

3. Quilt as desired.

4. Bind the quilt.

All in the Family

FINISHED BLOCK SIZE: 9″ × 9″ • FINISHED QUILT SIZE: 77″ × 99½″

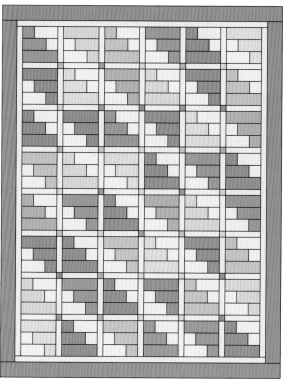

All in the Family quilt layout options

Increase the size of this quilt easily, just by adding borders! This size is great for a twin bed, with enough length to cover the pillow and hang over the sides of the bed. It is also a generous coverlet for a king-size bed.

MATERIALS

Follow the materials list for *Steps and Stairs* (page 120) except:

- **Cream:** 3⅔ yards for blocks, sashing, and inner border

- **Red:** 1½ yards for outer border

- **Binding:** ⅞ yard

- **Backing:** 2½ yards of 108″-wide fabric *or* 6 yards of 44″-wide fabric

- **Batting:** 86″ × 108″

CUTTING

Follow the cutting instructions for *Steps and Stairs* (page 121), except:

CREAM

- Cut 8 strips 2½″ × WOF.

RED

- Cut 9 strips 5″ × WOF.

BINDING

- Cut 10 strips 2½″ × WOF for double-fold binding.

INSTRUCTIONS

All seam allowances are ¼". Follow the instructions for Steps and Stairs Block Assembly and Quilt Construction. After sewing together the quilt top, add the borders.

BORDERS

1. Piece together the inner border strips end to end using diagonal seams. Measure the length of the quilt *through the center* and cut 2 inner border pieces to this length. Sew the inner border strips to each long side of the quilt. Press the seam allowance toward the inner border strip.

2. Measure the width of the quilt *through the center* and cut 2 inner border pieces to this same measurement. Sew the strips to the top and bottom of the quilt as shown in *All in the Family* quilt layout diagram (page 123).

3. Repeat Steps 1–2 to apply the outer border strips.

QUILTING AND FINISHING

Follow the instructions for *Steps and Stairs* Quilting and Finishing (page 122).

Jane's Favorite

FINISHED BLOCK SIZE: 9" × 9" • FINISHED QUILT SIZE: 54½" × 72½"

Jane's Favorite quilt layout

This variation has no sashing or borders, so it goes together very quickly. This quilt is made up of only fat quarters, so it can easily be made with a precut fat quarter bundle.

MATERIALS

- **Medium or dark:** 12 fat quarters
- **Cream or light:** 6 fat quarters
- **Binding:** ⅝ yard
- **Backing:** 3½ yards
- **Batting:** 62" × 78"

CUTTING

WOF = width of fabric

MEDIUM OR DARK

Follow the cutting instructions for the medium or dark fat quarters in *Steps and Stairs* (page 121). Do not cut cornerstones.

From each of the 6 fat quarters:

- Cut 4 strips 3½″ × 20″.

  Subcut each strip into 2 squares 3½″ × 3½″ and 2 rectangles 3½″ × 6½″.

- Sort the squares and rectangles into 48 matching pairs of 1 square and 1 rectangle.

BINDING

- Cut 7 strips 2½″ × WOF for double-fold binding.

INSTRUCTIONS

All seam allowances are ¼″.

BLOCK ASSEMBLY

Follow the instructions for Steps and Stairs *Block Assembly (page 121). Use matching fabrics in each block.*

QUILT CONSTRUCTION

Arrange the blocks in 8 horizontal rows, with 6 blocks in each row. This quilt pattern has a variety of fun layouts. Here are a few variations you might like:

Layout options without borders or sashing

QUILTING AND FINISHING

Follow the instructions for *Steps and Stairs* Quilting and Finishing (page 122).

Stephanie's Choice

FINISHED BLOCK SIZE: 9" × 9" • FINISHED QUILT SIZE: 54½" × 72½"

Stephanie's Choice quilt layout

Here's a version of *Steps and Stairs* with more light in the blocks because there is less dark fabric.

MATERIALS

- **Light:** 12 fat quarters
- **Medium or dark:** 6 fat quarters
- **Binding:** ⅝ yard
- **Backing:** 3½ yards
- **Batting:** 62" × 78"

CUTTING

WOF = width of fabric

LIGHT

- Follow the cutting instructions for the medium or dark fat quarters in *Steps and Stairs* (page 121).

MEDIUM OR DARK

- Follow the cutting instructions for the cream or light fat quarters in *Jane's Favorite* (page 125).

INSTRUCTIONS

BLOCK ASSEMBLY

1. Sew a light square 3½" × 3½" to a dark strip 3½" × 6½". Sew the matching light 3½" × 6½" strip to a dark square 3½" × 3½". Press toward the darker fabric. Repeat for all 48 matching sets of fabric.

2. Arrange the block as shown in the block layout diagram. Add a matching light-colored strip 3½" × 9½" to the bottom and sew together the units lengthwise. Press the seam allowances in the same direction. Make 48 blocks.

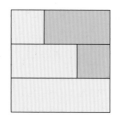

Stephanie's Choice block layout

QUILT CONSTRUCTION

Arrange the blocks in 8 horizontal rows, with 6 blocks in each row. Play with your block arrangement to find different ways to arrange your quilt!

Another *Stephanie's Choice* quilt arrangement with light-colored blocks

QUILTING AND FINISHING

Follow the instructions for *Steps and Stairs* Quilting and Finishing (page 122).

Jack's Wish

FINISHED BLOCK SIZE: 9" × 9" • FINISHED QUILT SIZE: 68½" × 86½"

Jack's Wish quilt layout

Make any of the above variations with no sashing and easily increase the size with a border. This one is sized for a twin bed.

MATERIALS

Follow the materials list for *Jane's Favorite* (page 124), except:

- **Orange:** ⅔ yard for inner border
- **Gray:** 1⅜ yards for outer border
- **Binding:** ⅔ yard
- **Backing:** 5½ yards
- **Batting:** 76" × 94"

CUTTING

WOF = width of fabric

ORANGE
- Cut 7 strips 2½" × WOF for inner border.

GRAY
- Cut 8 strips 5½" × WOF for outer border.

BINDING
- Cut 8 strips 2½" × WOF for double-fold binding.

INSTRUCTIONS

All seam allowances are ¼". Follow the instructions for Steps and Stairs Block Assembly and Quilt Construction (page 121). After sewing together the quilt top, add the borders.

BORDERS

Follow the instructions for *All in the Family* Borders (page 124).

QUILTING AND FINISHING

Follow the instructions for *Steps and Stairs* Quilting and Finishing (page 122).

About the Designer

Photo by Bob Pfau

SUE PFAU has always loved creating things and working with her hands. After years of doing cross-stitch, crocheting, and knitting, she started quilting when she was 32 years old and has been designing patterns for five years. She gears her patterns for precuts and makes her fabric requirements very simple. "I like to use precut fabrics because I don't like picking out the fabric colors and prints myself," she said. Plus, being a busy mom, I like uncomplicated designs that go together quickly." She is the author of *Quilts from Sweet Jane*, featuring quilt designs from precuts. Check out her patterns on Etsy or read her blog, Sweet Jane's (sweetjanesquilting.blogspot.com).